The Power Of a Woman's Words

SHARON JAYNES

HARVEST HOUSE PUBLISHERS
EUGENE, OREGON

Cover design by Bryce Williamson

Cover photo © Miroslav Boskov, IMR, GOLDsquirrel, letoosen / Gettyimages

The Power of a Woman's Words (revised)
Copyright © 2007, 2020 by Sharon Jaynes
Published by Harvest House Publishers
Eugene, Oregon 97408
www.harvesthousepublishers.com

ISBN 978-0-7369-7983-2 (pbk.)
ISBN 978-0-7369-7984-9 (eBook)

Library of Congress Cataloging-in-Publication Data
Jaynes, Sharon.
The power of a woman's words / Sharon Jaynes. p. cm.
ISBN 978-0-7369-1869-5 (pbk.)
ISBN 978-0-7369-3502-9 (eBook)

1. Influence (Psychology)—Religious aspects—Christianity. 2. Oral communication—Religious aspects—Christianity. 3. Christian women—Conduct of life. I. Title.
BV4597.53.I52J39 2007
248.8'43—dc22
2007007378
Library of Congress Control Number: 2019957948

Printed in the United States of America

20 21 22 23 24 25 26 / BP-SK / 10 9 8 7 6 5 4 3 2

To my precious friend Cynthia Price,
a woman who uses her words well.

Cynthia,
Many friends may come and go,
But rare the whole life through,
Are those who are forever friends,
Like the friend I've found in you.

Acknowledgments

Just as a painting combines many colors on a canvas to create what the artist intended, this manuscript combines many lives to create a portrait of *The Power of a Woman's Words*. I am so thankful for Jean Harper, Gayle Wentling, Catherine Grimes, Mary Marshal Young, Connie Roads, Gayle Roper, Glynnis Whitwer, Don and Jona Wright, Nancy Anderson, Mary Southerland, Bonnie Schulte, Mary Johnson, Sharon Johnston, Jonathan Edwards, Ginny Carlson, Larry Clark, and Kim Moore for sharing your stories of how you were impacted by a woman's words. The examples you shared help us all to see the impact our words have on those around us.

I am forever grateful to the staff of Harvest House Publishers. It is such an honor to work with this incredible team of men and women who truly are bringing in a harvest for God. Thank you, Bob Hawkins Jr., Terry Glaspey, and LaRae Weikert, for believing in the project; and Kim Moore and Kathleen Kerr for their expertise in editing.

And to my Girlfriends in God, Mary Southerland and Gwen Smith—I am so thankful that God has joined us together for such a time as this to share not only our words but our lives as well.

While this book is about the power of a woman's words, it is the power of a man's words that has been the wind beneath my wings along this entire journey. Thank you, Steve, my wonderful husband, for giving me the encouragement I've needed, for believing in me, and for praying for me each step of the way. I am also so thankful for my son, Steven, an amazing man whom God has used as a reflector of my words.

Finally, and most importantly, I am so thankful to my Savior, Jesus Christ. It is only by God's grace that I am allowed to reach out to His children by the written word.

To God be the glory!

Contents

PART ONE

The Power
We Possess

1

Mixed Messages

Discretion of speech is more than eloquence.

FRANCIS BACON

My friend Catherine and I set out for a lazy summer stroll through the neighborhood just before the fireflies emerged to start their party. We chatted about raising boys, working husbands, and decorating dilemmas. When we arrived back at her house, she invited me to come in and look at some fabric swatches for a new sofa. Before I knew it, a few minutes had turned into a few hours.

"Oh, my!" I exclaimed. "It's ten o'clock. I've been gone for over two hours! I bet Steve's worried sick. He doesn't even know where I am. I'd better give him a call before I start back home."

When I dialed our number, the answering machine picked up. After I listened to my sweet Southern greeting, I left a bitter message.

"Steve, I was calling to let you know I'm at Catherine's. I thought you'd be worried, but apparently you don't even care because you won't even pick up the phone!" Click. I said my goodbyes to Catherine and left feeling dejected. "I'm wandering around in the dark all alone and he doesn't even care," I mumbled to no one in particular. "I could be lying in a ditch injured, or dead for that matter! He doesn't even care. I don't think he even loves me."

As my eyes adjusted to the darkness, I noticed someone coming toward me. It was Prince Charming riding on his steed! Actually, it was Steve riding on his bicycle.

"Where have you been?" Steve desperately asked. "I've been riding all over the neighborhood looking for you! Do you know what time it is?"

"Oh, you do care," I said with a grin, giving him a big hug.

"What are you talking about?"

"Oh, nothing. Let's go home."

When we arrived at the house, what did I do? You know it, girl-friend; I quickly erased the message on the answering machine before Steve could hear my caustic words. *Whew*, I thought. *That was close.*

A few days later, Steve called me from work.

"Sharon, have you listened to the answering machine lately?"

"No, why?"

"Well, I think there's something on there you need to hear."

We hung up and I reached for my cell phone to call my landline phone. The message on the answering machine went something like this:

(The voice of sweet Southerness) "Hello, you've reached the Jaynes' residence. We're unable to answer the phone right now… (enter the voice of Cruella De Vil) "I was calling to let you know I'm at Catherine's. I thought you'd be worried, but apparently you don't even care because you won't even pick up the phone!" (Return of sweet Southerness) "At the sound of the beep, leave a message, and we'll get back with you as soon as possible." Beep.

"Oh, my goodness!" I screamed. "How did this happen! How many people have heard this over the past three days?"

I called the phone company, and they explained that sometimes during a thunderstorm (which had occurred three days prior), lightning strikes the wires and answering machine messages get scrambled. My message somehow became attached to the greeting.

I was mortified. It sounded like Dr. Jekyll and Mrs. Hyde.

"Lord," I prayed, "this is so embarrassing."

"Yes, it is," He replied.

Well, He didn't really *say* that in so many words. It was more like this: "With the tongue we praise our Lord and Father, and with it we curse human beings, who have been made in God's likeness. Out of the same mouth come praise and cursing. My brothers and sisters, this should not be. Can both fresh water and salt water flow from the same spring? My brothers and sisters, can a fig tree bear olives, or a grapevine bear figs? Neither can a salt spring produce fresh water" (James 3:9-12). As my country grandma would say, that means what's down in the well will come up in the bucket.

"Okay, Lord, I get the message." But, unfortunately, so did a lot of other people.

I am amazed how quickly we women can flit back and forth between blessing and belittling, praising and putting down, cheering and critiquing—all in a matter of seconds. God has given us incredible power in our sphere of influence, and it begins with the words we speak. Few forces have greater impact than the utterances that pass our lips. Our words can embolden a child to accomplish great feats, encourage a husband to conquer the world, reignite the dying embers of a friend's broken dreams, cheer on a fellow believer to run the race of life, and draw a lost soul to Christ. Words start wars and bring peace—globally, and right in our own homes.

I am so glad you've joined me on this journey to one of the most powerful gifts that God has given each of us—words. We'll discover how we shape the lives of others with words that speak life into the human soul or suck the life right out of them. In addition to looking at how our words impact those we come in contact with every day, we'll also look at various women in the Bible and how their words influenced generations after them. We'll explore the power available to each of us to harness this mighty force and use it for good. Most importantly, we'll join hands and hearts and discover how to change the words we speak to become the women God intended all along.

Are words powerful? Yes! Just how powerful? We'll learn together. Let's take a look at one of God's most incredible gifts to mankind and consider the potential we have right under our noses...words.

2
God's Incredible Gift

The Bible has a lot to say about our mouths,
our lips, our tongues, for our speech betrays us.
What is down in the well will come up in the bucket.

VANCE HAVNER

God has given us a valuable treasure—this gift of words, and with great riches comes great responsibility. The gift wasn't meant to be ill-used for selfish gratification, but invested in others for their edification. Speaking life not only changes that one person we're speaking to, but can affect generations that follow. Miss Thompson, a schoolteacher who taught fifth grade, saw firsthand how an encouraging word can change the course of a day...the course of a life. Here's her story as written by Elizabeth Ballard:

THREE LETTERS FROM TEDDY[1]

Teddy's letter came today and now that I've read it, I will place it in my cedar chest with the other things that are important to my life.

"I wanted you to be the first to know."

I smiled as I read the words he had written, and my heart swelled with a pride that I had no right to feel. *Teddy Stallard*. I have not seen Teddy Stallard since he was a student in my fifth-grade class, 15 years ago.

I'm ashamed to say that from the first day he stepped into my classroom, I disliked Teddy. Teachers try hard not to have favorites in a class, but we try even harder not to show dislike for a child, any child.

Nevertheless, every year there are one or two children that one cannot help but be attached to, for teachers are human, and it is human nature to like bright, pretty, intelligent people, whether they are ten years old or 25. And sometimes, not too often, fortunately, there will be one or two students to whom the teacher just can't seem to relate.

I had thought myself quite capable of handling my personal feelings along that line until Teddy walked into my life. There wasn't a child I particularly liked that year, but Teddy was most assuredly one I disliked.

He was a dirty little boy. Not just occasionally, but all the time. His hair hung low over his ears, and he actually had to hold it out of his eyes as he wrote his papers in class. (And this was before it was fashionable to do so!) Too, he had a peculiar odor about him that I could never identify.

Yes, his physical faults were many, but his intellect left a lot to be desired. By the end of the first week I knew he was hopelessly behind the others. Not only was he behind, he was just plain slow! I began to withdraw from him immediately.

Any teacher will tell you that it's more of a pleasure to teach a bright child. It is definitely more rewarding for one's ego. But any teacher worth his or her credentials can channel work to the bright child, keeping that child challenged and learning, while the major effort is with the slower ones. Any teacher *can* do this. Most teachers *do,* but I didn't. Not that year.

In fact, I concentrated on my best students and let the others follow along as best they could. Ashamed as I am to admit it, I took perverse pleasure in using my red pen; and each time I came to Teddy's papers, the cross-marks (and they were many) were always a little larger and a little redder than necessary.

"Poor work!" I would write with a flourish.

While I did not actually ridicule the boy, my attitude was obviously quite apparent to the class, for he quickly became the class "goat," the outcast—the unlovable and the unloved.

He knew I didn't like him, but he didn't know why. Nor did I know—then or now—why I felt such an intense dislike for him. All I know is that he was a little boy no one cared about, and I made no effort on his behalf.

The days rolled by and we made it through the Fall Festival, the Thanksgiving holidays, and I continued marking happily with my red pen. As our Christmas break approached, I knew that Teddy would never catch up in time to be promoted to the sixth-grade level. He would be a repeater.

To justify myself, I went to his cumulative folder from time to time. He had very low grades for the first four years, but no grade failure. How he had made it, I didn't know. I closed my mind to the personal remarks:

First Grade: "Teddy shows promise by work and attitude, but he has a poor home situation."

Second Grade: "Teddy could do better. Mother terminally ill. He receives little help at home."

Third Grade: "Teddy is a pleasant boy. Helpful, but too serious. Slow learner. Mother passed away end of the year."

Fourth Grade: "Very slow but well behaved. Father shows no interest."

Well, they passed him four times, but he will certainly repeat fifth grade! Do him good! I said to myself.

And then the last day before the holidays arrived. Our little tree on the reading table sported paper and popcorn chains. Many gifts were heaped underneath, waiting for the big moment.

Teachers always get several gifts at Christmas, but mine that year seemed bigger and more elaborate than ever. There was not a student who had not brought me one. Each unwrapping brought squeals of delight, and the proud giver would receive effusive thank-yous.

His gift wasn't the last one I picked up. In fact it was in the middle of the pile. Its wrapping was a brown paper bag, and he had colored Christmas trees and red bells all over it. It was stuck together with masking tape. "For Miss Thompson—From Teddy."

The group was completely silent and I felt conspicuous, embarrassed because they all stood watching me unwrap that gift. As I removed the last bit of masking tape, two items fell to my desk. A gaudy rhinestone bracelet with several stones missing and a small bottle of dime-store cologne—half empty. I could hear the snickers and whispers, and I wasn't sure I could look at Teddy.

"Isn't this lovely?" I asked, placing the bracelet on my wrist. "Teddy, would you help me fasten it?"

He smiled shyly as he fixed the clasp, and I held up my wrist for all of them to admire. There were a few hesitant *ooh*'s and *ahh*'s, but, as I dabbed the cologne behind my ears, all the little girls lined up for a dab behind their ears.

I continued to open the gifts until I reached the bottom of the pile. We ate our refreshments until the bell rang. The children filed out with shouts of "See you next year!" and "Merry Christmas!" but Teddy waited at his desk.

When they had all left, he walked toward me clutching his gift and books to his chest.

"You smell just like Mom," he said softly. "Her bracelet looks real pretty on you too. I'm glad you liked it."

He left quickly and I locked the door, sat down at my desk and wept, resolving to make up to Teddy what I had deliberately deprived him of—a teacher who cared.

I stayed every afternoon with Teddy from the day class resumed on January 2 until the last day of school. Sometimes we worked together. Sometimes he worked alone while I drew up lesson plans or graded papers. Slowly but surely he caught up with the rest of the class. Gradually there was a definite upward curve in his grades.

He did not have to repeat the fifth grade. In fact, his final averages were among the highest in the class, and although I knew he would be moving out of the state when school was out, I was not worried for him. Teddy had reached a level that would stand him in good stead the following year, no matter where he went. He had enjoyed a measure of success, and as we were taught in our education courses: "Success builds success."

~

I did not hear from Teddy until several years later when his first letter appeared in my mailbox.

> *Dear Miss Thompson,*
>
> *I just wanted you to be the first to know. I will be graduating second in my class on May 25 from E_____ High School.*
>
> > *Very truly yours,*
> > *Teddy Stallard*

I sent him a card of congratulations and a small package, a pen and pencil set. I wondered what he would do after graduation. I found out four years later when Teddy's second letter came.

> *Dear Miss Thompson,*
>
> *I was just informed today that I'll be graduating first in my class. The university has been a little tough but I'll miss it.*
>
> > *Very truly yours,*
> > *Teddy Stallard*

I sent him a good pair of sterling silver monogrammed cuff links and a card, so proud of him I could burst!

And now—today—Teddy's third letter:

> *Dear Miss Thompson,*
>
> *I wanted you to be the first to know. As of today I am Theodore J. Stallard, MD. How about that???!!!*
>
> *I'm going to be married on July 27, and I'm hoping you can come and sit where Mom would sit if she were here. I'll have no family there as Dad died last year.*
>
> > *Very truly yours,*
> > *Ted Stallard*

I'm not sure what kind of gift one sends to a doctor on completion of medical school. Maybe I'll just wait and take a wedding gift, but the note can't wait.

> *Dear Ted,*
>
> *Congratulations! You made it and you did it yourself! In spite of those like me and not because of us, this day has come for you.*
>
> *God bless you. I'll be at that wedding with bells on!!!*

Miss Thompson changed the course of one little boy's life. She gave Teddy words that built him up when he felt as though life had knocked him down for good. Can't you hear her now? "Great job, Teddy!" "You can do it!" She became the wind beneath his wings when he felt as though he had been grounded from flight. And years later, she had a front row seat as she watched him soar into his future. That is the power of a woman's words. An incredible gift God has given those created in His very image. You and me!

Words weren't meant to be ill-used for selfish gratification, but invested in others for their edification.

AND GOD SAID

"In the beginning God created the heavens and the earth" (Genesis 1:1). That seems like a splendid place for us to start our journey—at the beginning of time. When God created the world and stocked the seas with marine life and the skies with winged creatures—when He caused the stars to ignite the night sky and placed the sun to light the day and the moon to illumine the darkness—He did so with words. "*And God said,* 'Let there be light.'" "*And God said,* 'Let there be a vault between the waters to separate water from water.'" "*And God said,* 'Let the water

under the sky be gathered to one place, and let dry ground appear.'"
"*And God said*, 'Let there be lights in the vault of the sky to separate
the day from the night.'" "*And God said*, 'Let the water teem with living creatures, and let birds fly above the earth across the vault of the
sky.'" "*And God said*, 'Let the land produce living creatures according
to their kinds.'" "*Then God said*, 'Let us make mankind in our image,
in our likeness, so that they may rule over the fish in the sea and the
birds in the sky, over the livestock and all the wild animals, and over all
the creatures that move along the ground.'" And it was so. (See Genesis 1:3-26.) God spoke, and what was not became what is. When God
created the heavens and the earth, He used a mighty force—words. "By
the word of the Lord the heavens were made, their starry host by the
breath of his mouth" (Psalm 33:6).

Amazingly, when God created mankind in His own image, He gave
us that same powerful ability to speak words. He didn't entrust words
to zebras, birds, monkeys, elephants, lizards, or horses. He entrusted
words to mere mortals. Our words also have creative potential. They
can light up a child's face disheartened by discouragement, lessen the
burdens of a husband weighed down with worries, lift the spirits a
friend who feels dejected by life, cheer on brothers and sisters in Christ
to grow in grace, and bring the message of the hope and healing of Jesus
Christ to a wounded world. Words are one of the most powerful forces
in the universe, and amazingly, God has entrusted them to you and me.
Words become the mirror in which others see themselves.

I've always been amazed at the power in a tiny atom too small to be
seen by the naked eye. Fission (splitting the nucleus of an atom) and
fusion (joining nuclei together) have the potential to generate enough
power to provide energy for an entire city or enough destructive potential to level an entire town. It all depends on how and when the joining together or splitting apart takes place.

So it is with our words. Bound in one small group of muscles called
the tongue lies an instrument with huge potential for good or evil, to
build up or to tear down, to empower or devour, to heal or to hurt. It
all depends on how and when the joining together and splitting apart
take place. Our words can make or break a marriage, paralyze or propel

a friend, sew together or tear apart a relationship, build up or bury a dream, curse God or confess Christ. And even though the tongue has no bones, it is strong enough to break someone's heart.

Just as God used words to create physical life, our words can be the spark to generate spiritual life. Paul taught, "If you declare with your mouth, 'Jesus is Lord,' and believe in your heart that God raised him from the dead, you will be saved. For it is with your heart that you believe and are justified, and it is *with your mouth that you profess your faith and are saved*" (Romans 10:9-10). Wow! It is with our mouth that we are saved. That is incredible power right below our nose.

The words *talk, tongue, speak, speech, words, mouth,* and *silence* are used over 3,500 times in the Bible. Words that are used by men and women just like you and me. Some are examples of the damage words can cause, and some are examples of the life they can bring. We read about women who gossiped, whined, lied, manipulated, taunted, and caused many to stumble. We also read about women who encouraged, prophesied, saved lives, instructed warriors, and caused many to walk in truth. Some did both. You and I probably will too.

Just as we read the words, "And God said," one day people will say the same about us. "And she said…"

"By the word of the lord the heavens were made, their starry host by the breath of his mouth" (Psalm 33:6).

RUDDERS, BRIDLES, AND FOREST FIRES

In the Bible, James paints a poignant picture of the power of our words:

> When we put bits into the mouths of horses to make them obey us, we can turn the whole animal. Or take ships as an example. Although they are so large and are driven by

strong winds, they are steered by a very small rudder wherever the pilot wants to go. Likewise, the tongue is a small part of the body, but it makes great boasts. Consider what a great forest is set on fire by a small spark. The tongue also is a fire, a world of evil among the parts of the body. It corrupts the whole body, *sets the whole course of one's life on fire,* and is itself set on fire by hell (James 3:3-6).

The ESV Study Bible notes: "The tongue is one of the smaller organs in the body, yet it has control over everything a person is and does. The tongue, 'sets the whole course of his life, (literally "the cycle of existence") likely means the "ups and downs" of life.' The tongue turns upside down every aspect of life in the community as well as in the individual."[2]

An average horse weighs 840 to 2,200 pounds. That's a big bulk of bone and muscle. And yet, a small piece of metal lying across the horse's tongue, attached to a bridle in the rider's hand, controls whether the horse moves to the left or the right. Pulling the bridle toward the rider signals the horse to stop, and slacking the bridle signals the horse to move ahead. Just to think that such a large animal is controlled by such a small piece of metal pressing against its tongue is mind-boggling.

I love how Peterson paraphrases James 3:3-6 in his work The Message (MSG):

A bit in the mouth of a horse controls the whole horse. A small rudder on a huge ship in the hands of a skilled captain sets a course in the face of the strongest winds. A word out of your mouth may seem of no account, but *it can accomplish nearly anything—or destroy it!*

It only takes a spark, remember, to set off a forest fire. A careless or wrongly placed word out of your mouth can do that. By our speech we can ruin the world, turn harmony to chaos, throw mud on a reputation, send the whole world up in smoke, and go up in smoke with it—smoke right from the pit of hell.

On November 23, 2016, just such a spark ignited in the Great

Smoky Mountains National Park. The wildfire began on a steep, rug-
ged peak known as Chimney Tops, about four miles from Gatlinburg,
Tennessee. The fire burned for several days, mostly in the unreachable
peaks of the Great Smoky Mountains National Park, not far from the
edge of one of the most popular hiking trails. The fire was small and so
remote that for days firefighters couldn't get to it. Instead, they came
up with a plan to contain it. But beginning Sunday afternoon and into
Monday morning, the moisture vanished from the air, the temperature rose, and the wind began galloping through the trees. By Monday
afternoon, there was no stopping the hungry flames.[3]

Aided by strong wind gusts up to 76 miles per hour and months
of parching drought, the blaze sprinted toward the populated tourist
attraction of Gatlinburg. At 5 p.m., there were no fires in Gatlinburg.
Within one hour, 20 buildings were ablaze.[4]

For days, 780 firefighting personnel from several states fought wildfires that shut down the city of Gatlinburg at the height of its winter
tourism. The blaze damaged or destroyed more than 2,400 homes and
businesses. Fourteen people died, 134 were injured. Both local resi-
dents and visitors were among the dead. Many homeowners returned
home to find all they owned in ashes. Sevier County and 17,000 acres
of woodland were left a scarred and charred piece of earth. And it
started with a careless spark.

Two teenage boys were horsing around with matches on a popular hiking trail. Another hiker apparently captured an image of the boys
walking away from the trail with smoke in the background. Authorities
were able to identify the boys by their clothes, and they were later arrested.

One match.

One spark.

Two careless people.

On average more than 100,000 wildfires destroy 4 to 5 million
acres in the U.S. annually. In 2018, 52,303 wildfires destroyed 8.5
million acres. About 90 percent are believed to have been caused by
human carelessness, and 10 percent by natural causes, such as lightning strikes.

While forest fires leave naked trees and barren hillsides that take years to revive, lives singed by fiery words can be laid bare forever. We would never carelessly fling a lit match out of a car window while passing a national forest, and yet many times we carelessly toss fiery words about as we pass through life.

The writer of Proverbs notes, "Death and life are in the power of the tongue" (Proverbs 18:21 NASB). Of all the spiritual disciplines, I believe bringing our tongues under the submission of the Holy Spirit is one of the greatest. Why? Because through our words we bring death and through our words we bring life.

There is a story told about Xanthus the philosopher. He once told his servant he was going to have some friends for dinner the following evening and instructed him to get the best thing he could find in the market. When the philosopher and his guests sat down the next day at the table, they had nothing but tongue—four or five courses of tongue cooked in various ways. The philosopher finally lost his patience and said to his servant, "Didn't I tell you to get the best thing in the market?" The servant said, "I did get the best thing in the market. Isn't the tongue the organ of sociability, the organ of eloquence, the organ of kindness, the organ of worship?"

Then Xanthus said, "Tomorrow I want you to get the worst thing in the market." The next day when the philosopher sat at the table, there was nothing but tongue—four or five courses of tongue—tongue in this shape and in that shape. The philosopher lost his patience again and said, "Didn't I tell you to get the worst thing in the market?" The servant replied, "I did; for isn't the tongue the organ of blasphemy, the organ of defamation, the organ of lying?"[5]

I have never eaten tongue before, but I have had to eat my words. While words are one of God's most incredible gifts, in the wrong hands—or rather, in the wrong mouth—they possess destructive potential. Our words are powerful, and they have consequences.

Words become the mirror in which others see themselves.

LOOKING FOR A SAFE HARBOR

One day I was glancing through an insert in my local newspaper called *The Mecklenburg Neighbor*. A calendar of events for the week was listed on the last two pages. Entry after entry mentioned support group meetings: Adoptive Parents Support Group, Adult Children of Alcoholics Support Group, Alzheimer's Disease Support Group, Dementia Caregivers Support Group, Amputee Support Group, Breast-feeding Support Group, Codependents Anonymous, Eating Disorders Anonymous, Emotions Anonymous, Gamblers Anonymous, Headaches Anonymous, Moms of Multiples, Sex Addicts Anonymous...All in all, 146 support group meetings were scheduled in my fair city in one week. A boxed message was posted above the upper right-hand column: "If you are looking for a support group not mentioned here, give us a call and we'll find one for you."

I closed the newspaper with a knot in the pit of my stomach. How desperately men and women long for an encouraging word. They need a cheerleader to tell them, "You can do it. Don't give up!" They long for a fellow journeyman to bolster them up when the road is too arduous to travel alone. They yearn for teammates to rally behind them, reminding them they are not isolated in this game called life.

Years ago there were no such things as support groups. Rather, we had family or neighbors who helped when burdens became too difficult to bear alone. Women talked over the fence as they raised children together. They canned vegetables together when the crops came in. They stitched quilts to keep bodies warm and chatted to keep their hearts warm. But times have changed. Many of us don't even know our next-door neighbors' names, our families live across several state lines, and we've lost that sense of community that was the mainstay just a few generations ago. Where once we had a welcome mat at our front doors, now we have warning stickers to let those who approach our homes know we have an alarm system. And if you're like me, you have both welcome and warning, which I'm sure is very confusing.

This lack of connection is prevalent in our Christian community as well. A few years ago, I was in a couples' Bible study. One man in the group had only been a Christian for a short time. "You know what I miss most since I became a Christian?" he asked. "I miss hanging out at bars. I miss talking with other men and just being real."

His confession broke my heart. Rob didn't miss the alcohol. He missed the fellowship where no one would judge, condemn, or make him feel guilty. The bar was a safe place. I read something a few years ago that reminded me of Rob's confession:

> The neighborhood bar is possibly the best counterfeit there is to the fellowship Christ wants to give His church. It's an imitation, dispensing liquor instead of grace, escape rather than reality, but it's permissive, accepting, and inclusive fellowship. It is unshockable. It is democratic. You can tell people secrets and they usually don't tell others or even want to. The bar flourishes not because most people are alcoholics, but because God has put into the human heart the desire to know and be known, to love and be loved, and so many seek a counterfeit at the price of a few beers.[6]

Why do spouses stop by the neighborhood bar before heading home? Could it be the same reason teenagers prefer peers over parents, the same reason church hoppers bounce from one church to the next, or the same reason hurting people attend support groups instead of sharing their struggles among friends? Could it be they are looking for a safe harbor, an uplifting word, a verbal pat on the back—grace for the grumpy, safety for the storm-tossed, and rest for the bone-weary? I've never met anyone yet who didn't need a kind word. People need a place where they can set anchor without fear of pirates coming aboard and robbing them blind. I believe we can be that "safe place." We can learn to speak words of grace that invite those around us to come ashore for a needed respite and then set sail once the storm has passed.

A SIMPLE CHOICE
WITH LASTING RESULTS

We are shaped by words from those who love us or refuse to love us. We are shaped by the words of those who don't even know our names.

It is the heart cry of all mankind to be loved and accepted, and sometimes a simple word of encouragement can make all the difference. William Barclay said,

> One of the highest of human duties is the duty of encouragement. It is easy to laugh at men's ideals; it is easy to pour cold water on their enthusiasm; it is easy to discourage others. The world is full of discouragers. We have a Christian duty to encourage one another. Many a time a word of praise or thanks or appreciation or cheer has kept a man on his feet. Blessed is the man [or woman] who speaks such a word.[7]

What exactly is encouragement? My dictionary defines it "to give courage or confidence to; to raise the hopes of; to help on by sympathetic advice and interest; to advise and make it easy for [someone to do something] to promote or stimulate; to strengthen." In contrast, discouragement is "to say or take away the courage of, to deter, to lessen enthusiasm for and so restrict or hinder."

Amazingly, our words have the capacity for both, and we are faced with the choice every time we speak as to which it will be. The Hebrew word for "mouth," *peh*, is often translated "edge."[8] Like a knife, the tongue has a sharp, powerful edge that can either be used to hurt or heal. A knife in the hands of a skilled surgeon brings healing and life, but a knife in the hands of a murderer brings death. Like the surgeon, we can study how to use our mouths to bring life to those around us, and then make the simple choice to do just that.

How long does that one simple choice linger in someone's heart? How far-reaching are the echoes of a kind word? I believe the impact of a spoken or written word can remain long after our bodies have left this earth. Marie learned the lasting impact of words from a group of her students. Here is her story:

> He was in the first third-grade class I taught at Saint Mary's School in Morris, Minnesota. All thirty-four of my students were dear to me, but Mark Eklund was one in a

million. Very neat in appearance, he had that happy-to-be-alive attitude that made even his occasional mischievousness delightful.

Mark also talked incessantly. I had to remind him again and again that talking without permission was not acceptable. What impressed me so much, though, was his sincere response every time I had to correct him for misbehaving. "Thank you for correcting me, Sister!" I didn't know what to make of it at first, but before long I became accustomed to hearing it many times a day.

One morning my patience was growing thin when Mark talked once too often, and then I made a novice-teacher's mistake. I looked at Mark and said, "If you say one more word, I am going to tape your mouth shut!" It wasn't ten seconds later when Chuck blurted out, "Mark is talking again." I hadn't asked any of the students to help me watch Mark, but since I had stated the punishment in front of the class, I had to act on it.

I remember the scene as if it had occurred this morning. I walked to my desk, very deliberately opened the drawer, and took out a roll of masking tape. Without saying a word, I proceeded to Mark's desk, tore off two pieces of tape and made a big X with them over his mouth. I then returned to the front of the room.

As I glanced at Mark to see how he was doing, he winked at me. That did it! I started laughing. The class cheered as I walked back to Mark's desk, removed the tape, and shrugged my shoulders. His first words were, "Thank you for correcting me, Sister."

At the end of the year I was asked to teach junior high math. The years flew by, and before I knew it Mark was in my classroom again. He was more handsome than ever and just as polite. Since he had to listen carefully to my instruction in the "new math," he did not talk as much in ninth grade as he had in the third.

One Friday, things just didn't feel right. We had worked hard on a new concept all week, and I sensed that the students were growing frustrated with themselves and edgy with one another. I had to stop this crankiness before it got out of hand. So I asked them to list the names of the other students in the room on two sheets of paper, leaving a space between each name. Then I told them to think of the nicest thing they could say about each of their classmates and write it down.

It took the remainder of the class period to finish the assignment, and as the students left the room, each one handed me the papers. Charlie smiled. Mark said, "Thank you for teaching me, Sister. Have a good weekend."

That Saturday, I wrote down the name of each student on a separate sheet of paper, and I listed what everyone else had said about that individual. On Monday I gave each student his or her list. Before long, the entire class was smiling. "Really?" I heard whispered. "I never knew that meant anything to anyone!" "I didn't know others liked me so much!"

No one ever mentioned those papers in class again. I never knew if they discussed them after class or with their parents, but it didn't matter. The exercise had accomplished its purpose. The students were happy with themselves and with one another again.

That group of students moved on. Several years later, after I returned from vacation, my parents met me at the airport. As we were driving home, Mother asked the usual questions about the trip, the weather, my experiences in general. There was a slight lull in the conversation. Mother gave Dad a sideways glance and simply said, "Dad?" My father cleared his throat as he usually did before something important. "The Eklunds called last night," he began.

"Really?" I said. "I haven't heard from them in years. I wonder how Mark is."

Dad responded quietly. "Mark was killed in Vietnam," he said. "The funeral is tomorrow, and his parents would like it if you could attend." To this day I can still point to the exact spot on I-494 where Dad told me about Mark.

I had never seen a serviceman in a military coffin before. Mark looked so handsome, so mature. All I could think at that moment was *Mark, I would give all the masking tape in the world if only you would talk to me.*

The church was packed with Mark's friends. Chuck's sister sang "The Battle Hymn of the Republic." Why did it have to rain on the day of the funeral? It was difficult enough at the graveside. The pastor said the usual prayers, and the bugler played "Taps." One by one those who loved Mark took a last walk by the coffin.

I was the last one. As I stood there, one of the soldiers who had acted as pallbearer came up to me. "Were you Mark's math teacher?" he asked. I nodded as I continued to stare at the coffin. "Mark talked about you a lot," he said.

After the funeral, most of Mark's former classmates headed to Chuck's farmhouse for lunch. Mark's mother and father were there, obviously waiting for me. "We want to show you something," his father said, taking a wallet out of his pocket. "They found this on Mark when he was killed. We thought you might recognize it."

Opening the billfold, he carefully removed two worn pieces of notebook paper that had obviously been taped, folded, and refolded many times. I knew without looking that the papers were the ones on which I had listed all the good things each of Mark's classmates had said about him. "Thank you so much for doing that," Mark's mother said. "As you can see, Mark treasured it."

Mark's classmates started to gather around us. Charlie smiled rather sheepishly and said, "I still have my list. It's in the top drawer of my desk at home." Chuck's wife said,

"Chuck asked me to put his in our wedding album." "I have mine too," Marilyn said. "It's in my diary." Then Vicki, another classmate, reached into her pocketbook, took out her wallet, and showed her worn and frazzled list to the group. "I carry this with me at all times," Vicki said without batting an eyelash. "I think we all saved our lists."[9]

How long will our words echo in the hearts and minds of our children, our husbands, our friends, fellow believers, and the world? For all eternity, my friends. To the end of the age.

A Woman's Life-Changing Potential

*There is no more noble occupation in the world
than to assist another human being to succeed.*

ALAN LOY MCGINNIS

Have you ever met someone who just seems to take the wind out of your sails? You have a tiny spark of excitement, mention it to a friend, and then she aims the fire hose of discouraging words right at your hopes and dreams to douse your enthusiasm.

Susan was walking with a friend and sharing about an incredible experience she had on an airplane.

"I sat beside this young girl who had experienced so much trauma in her young life," Susan explained. "She had been abused as a child, neglected as a teen, and beaten by her boyfriend as a young adult. I know God placed us side by side on that flight. For two hours we talked, cried, and finally prayed together."

"Did you believe her?" the friend asked.

"Yes," Susan replied. "Why wouldn't I?"

"I don't know. I think sometimes people make up stories about their lives. Sometimes it's just too much to believe."

With those words, Susan's soaring spirits began a slow descent. Nothing makes a heart fly like bringing the hope and healing of Jesus Christ to a hurting heart. Susan had experienced that firsthand. She was still breathing in the crisp air of her mountaintop experience when the words of a friend rolled in like a dark cloud to rain down discouraging words that made Susan run for shelter. If the girl had made up her story, then Susan was a fool and the entire experience a farce.

Her desire for sharing the gospel in the future teetered on the careless words of an unthinking friend.

Have you ever noticed that there are certain people who bring out the best in others, and then there are certain people who tend to bring out the worst? I've heard them referred to as "attic people" and "basement people." One lifts you up; the other pulls you down.

I can think of people who seem to be the peroxide of the soul. Within minutes in their presence, all the impurities in my heart begin bubbling to the surface. It is not so much that I don't like the person. I just don't like the person I become when I am around them. There's just something about their words and tone that brings out the worst in me.

On the other hand, there are women I love to be around because I like who I am when I am with them. There's something about their words and tone that brings out the best in me. That sounds awfully selfish, doesn't it? But, honestly, who doesn't enjoy being around people who hold up an invisible mirror of acceptance and inspire us to be our best? The question is, which type of person do we want to be?

When we become women who expect the best in others and use our words to tell them so, they usually go to great lengths to meet our expectations. As women, we can determine to be gold miners who use our words to dig deep into a person's soul to unearth the treasures hidden below the surface. I have had such gold miners in my own life. I bet you have too.

For most of my life I struggled with feelings of inferiority, insecurity, and inadequacy. But God sent various women with the hard hat of His love into my life to unearth treasures hidden beneath my protective shell. Mary Marshal Young helped me see who I really am as a child of God. She aimed the light of God's Word into the dark caverns of my soul to reveal the gold veins imbedded in the rocky crags of past hurts.

Gayle Roper read a few of my first stories and encouraged me not to give up on writing, even if I was met with rejection. "You have a gift," she said. "Don't give up when you are rejected. The difference between a writer and a published author is that the published author doesn't give up. You can do it. Press on!"

Before my first speaking engagement, my friend Lysa TerKeurst patted my shaking knees and said, "They are going to love you. Just tell them what you've been telling me every day."

Ginny had the opposite experience with her mother. When she was ten years old, her father died. This was hard on her because she always thought of him as her protector. *Who will love me the way I am? Who will love me for me?*

Ginny's older sister and younger brother were smart kids; they made the honor roll all the time. "You're not as smart as your sister," her mother remarked. "You'll never make the honor roll."

"We live up or down to the expectations people place on us," Ginny told me. "I did not make the honor roll until after my mother died. I was fifteen when she passed away, and after that I made the honor roll every time. While I missed my mom, with her low estimation of me removed I could blossom and grow into the woman God had intended all along. No longer did her negative words keep me down."

Every individual believes deep down that he or she has a greater capacity for success than they are currently experiencing. They simply need someone who will believe in them and tell them so—someone who will fan the flame rather than extinguish the fire. That person can be you.

Every individual believes deep down that he or she has a greater capacity for success than they are currently experiencing.

EMPOWERING OTHERS TO SUCCEED

Jesus was the Master of believing in the best in others and encouraging them to reach beyond their own limited view of their abilities. He did it for the little Zacchaeus, stubborn Martha, and especially His 12 best friends. His disciples had witnessed Jesus command a lame man to walk, restore the rotting skin of a leprous outcast, remove fever from Peter's mother-in-law, calm a raging storm, deliver a man from demons, and raise a little girl from the dead. But Jesus wanted more from His friends than to remain spectators in the gospel. He longed for them to be participants and partakers.

On a spring day shortly after the Passover celebration, Jesus retreated to the north shore of the Sea of Galilee. However, crowds of people quickly pursued this miracle worker to witness His teaching and healing power. As the sun began to sink toward the horizon, His disciples remarked that the people were growing hungry. Jesus turned to Philip and asked, "Where shall we buy bread for these people to eat?"

Jesus was not concerned with a lack of provisions. Rather, He was taking this opportunity to invite the disciples to share in His ministry. He didn't need their help. However, He wanted to invite them to participate in a miracle to boost their confidence and faith.

Philip was smart. In a matter of moments, he calculated that it would take eight months' wages to feed the ten thousand people gathered on the hill. But Jesus wasn't looking for facts; He was looking for faith.

Andrew was practical. He canvassed the crowd to see what resources were available...and he came back with five small barley cakes and two small fish. But Jesus wasn't looking for practical; He was looking for powerful.

Jesus told the disciples to have the crowd sit down in groups. Then He took the loaves and fish, blessed the food, and gave it to the disciples to distribute.

Did Jesus need the disciples' help? No. But He chose to include them in the miracle to let them know He believed in them. To empower them with confidence to carry on His work when He was gone.

Now, let's fast-forward a bit in Jesus's ministry. Like a coach who believes in his team, Jesus rallied the 12 and gave a rousing pep talk: "Go rather to the lost sheep of Israel. As you go, proclaim this message: 'The kingdom of heaven has come near.' Heal the sick, raise the dead, cleanse those who have leprosy, drive out demons. Freely you have received; freely give" (Matthew 10:6-8). In other words, "You can do it! I believe in you!"

Before His ascension, He gave them one last pep talk: "Go and make disciples of all nations, baptizing them in the name of the Father and of the Son and of the Holy Spirit, and teaching them to obey everything I have commanded you. And surely I am with you always, to the very end of the age" (Matthew 28:19-20). They had observed, learned, and practiced. Now it was time to step out into the world and spread the gospel without Jesus's physical presence. He believed in them, and He let them know it.

"Very truly I tell you," Jesus said, "whoever believes in me will do the works I have been doing, and they will do even greater things than these, because I am going to the Father" (John 14:12). Jesus wasn't simply encouraging the disciples by telling them they would have an even greater reach than He had; He was encouraging you and me as well. Because of the finished work of Jesus on the cross, and His Spirit in us, we can be the wind beneath the wings of those in our slice of life.

BECOMING THE WIND
BENEATH SOMEONE'S WINGS

Just as Jesus encouraged His disciples, and ultimately you and me, we can use our words to be the gentle wind beneath the wings of those in our slice of time. Jean Harper had such a woman in her life, and it changed everything. Let's ponder her story as told by Jean and Carol Kline.

Jean Harper was in the third grade when her teacher gave the class an assignment to write a report on what they wanted to be when they grew up. Jean's father was a crop duster pilot in the little farming community in Northern California where she was raised, and Jean was totally captivated by airplanes and flying. She poured her heart into her report and included all of her dreams; she wanted to crop dust, make parachute jumps, seed clouds and be an airline pilot. Her paper came back with an "F" on it. The teacher told her it was a "fairy tale" and that none of the occupations she listed were women's jobs. Jean was crushed and humiliated.

She showed her father the paper, and he told her that of course she could become a pilot. "Look at Amelia Earhart," he said. "That teacher doesn't know what she's talking about."

But as the years went by, Jean was beaten down by the discouragement and negativity she encountered whenever she talked about her career—"Girls can't become airline pilots; never have, never will. You're not smart enough, you're crazy. That's impossible."—until finally Jean gave up.

In her senior year of high school, her English teacher was a Mrs. Dorothy Slaton. Mrs. Slaton was an uncompromising, demanding teacher with high standards and a low tolerance for excuses. She refused to treat her students like children; instead, expecting them to behave like the responsible adults they would have to be to succeed in the real world after graduation. Jean was scared of her at first but grew to respect her firmness and fairness.

One day Mrs. Slaton gave the class an assignment. "What do you think you'll be doing ten years from now?" Jean thought about the assignment. *Pilot? No way. Flight attendant? I'm not pretty enough—they'd never accept me. Wife? What guy would want me? Waitress? I could do that.* That felt safe, so she wrote it down.

Mrs. Slaton collected the papers, and nothing more was said. Two weeks later, the teacher handed back the assignments, facedown on each desk, and asked this question: "If you had unlimited finances, unlimited access to the finest schools, unlimited talents and abilities, what would you do?" Jean felt a rush of the old enthusiasm, and with excitement she wrote down all her old dreams. When the students stopped writing, the teacher asked, "How many students wrote the same thing on both sides of the paper?" Not one hand went up.

The next thing that Mrs. Slaton said changed the course of Jean's life. The teacher leaned forward over her desk and said, "I have a little secret for you all. You do have unlimited abilities and talents. You *do* have access to the finest schools, and you *can* arrange for unlimited finances if you want something badly enough. This is it! When you leave school, if you don't go for your dreams, *no one* will do it for you. You can have what you want if you want it enough."

The hurt and fear of years of discouragement crumbled in the face of the truth of what Mrs. Slaton had said. Jean felt exhilarated and a little scared. She stayed after class and went up to the teacher's desk. Jean thanked Mrs. Slaton and told her about her dream of becoming a pilot. Mrs. Slaton half rose and slapped the desk top. "Then do it!" she said.

So Jean did. It didn't happen overnight. It took ten years of hard work, facing opposition that ranged from quiet skepticism to outright hostility. It wasn't in Jean's nature to stand up for herself when someone refused or humiliated her; instead, she would quietly try to find another way.

She became a private pilot and then got the necessary ratings to fly air freight and even commuter planes, but always as a copilot. Her employers were openly hesitant about promoting her because she was a woman. Even her father advised her to try something else. "It's impossible," he said. "Stop banging your head against the wall!"

But Jean answered, "Dad, I disagree. I believe that things are going to change, and I want to be at the head of the pack when they do."

Jean went on to do everything her third grade teacher said was a fairy tale—she did some crop dusting, made a few hundred parachute jumps, and even seeded clouds for a summer season as a weather modification pilot. In 1978, she became one of the first three female pilot trainees ever accepted by United Airlines and one of only 50 women airline pilots in the nation at the time. In 2013 *Captain* Jean Harper retired from United and piloted her last flight from Los Angeles to Denver. On board were her husband, Captain Victor Harper, their two children, and her mother. I know her teacher, Mrs. Slaton, would have been proud.

It was the power of one well-placed positive word, one spark of encouragement from a woman Jean respected that gave that uncertain young girl the strength and faith to pursue her dream. Today Jean says, "I chose to believe her."[1]

BRINGING OUT THE BEST IN OTHERS

Both vultures and hummingbirds are winged creatures. Vultures have a knack for finding dead and decaying animals because that is what they are looking for. Hummingbirds have a knack for spotting nectar in beautiful flowers because that is what they are looking for. When it comes to how we view other people, we'll most likely find what we're looking for. When we tell them the admirable qualities we see in them, they'll most likely strive to live up to our estimation.

I heard a story of a traveler nearing a great city. He stopped and asked a woman seated by the gas station, "What are the people like in the city?"

"How were the people where you came from?"

"A terrible bunch," the traveler responded. "Mean, untrustworthy, detestable in all respects."

"Ah," said the woman. "You will find them the same in the city ahead."

It wasn't too long after the first traveler pulled away that another car stopped and also asked about the people in the same city. Again the old woman asked about the people in the place the traveler had left.

"They were fine people; honest, industrious, and generous to a fault. I was sorry to leave," declared the second traveler.

"So you will find them in the city ahead," the wise woman smiled.

Years had taught the woman that we tend to see people through a lens of our own making. Whatever we're looking for is generally what we'll find.

Gayle experienced both the vultures and the hummingbirds in her own life. In the first grade she and her best friend, Jen, were reprimanded for talking in class. "If you two don't stop talking," the teacher scolded, "I'm going to tape your mouths shut!"

Later Jen whispered something to Gayle. "Shh," Gayle mouthed, not wanting to get in trouble.

The teacher never saw Jen speak, but she did see Gayle's lips move. Out came the tape. "I can still see her grinning behind those cat-glasses," Gayle recalled. "She didn't put tape over Jen's mouth, just mine. I was humiliated, and thus began my years of quiet shyness. I withdrew and felt scarred for many years to come."

A similar experience occurred in the third grade when Gayle was sent to the principal's office for correcting a teacher's spelling mistake on the chalkboard. Her insecurity was also compounded by words from her careless father. "You are so stupid!" he'd say. "Why are you so dumb? You'll never amount to anything!"

"I believed my dad," Gayle confided. "I thought I was a failure at everything. By the time I entered junior high, I was sad, lonely, afraid to trust people, and afraid to make new friends. I believed I was stupid and no good."

But something happened to turn Gayle's life around. She went off to college and lived with an amazing couple who showered affirmation on her battered and belittled self-image. Carole and Emmett spoke life into Gayle and rebuilt the ruins of her heart with kindness, love, and encouraging words. "I found myself dazed over the fact that people could be so kind, welcoming, and lovable toward me,"

Gayle remembered. "Oftentimes, I found myself wondering how one woman could have so many positive, encouraging words! Not once did Carole direct a negative word toward me. She believed in me and my abilities. Her positive words and actions stirred in me a desire to thrive in all areas of my life. I had always felt stupid, but with her encouragement as the wind beneath my wings, I soared to the top of my class. I realized I was not stupid after all. Like the scarecrow from *The Wizard of Oz,* I had a brain after all, but had never realized it until this wonderful woman pointed it out. It is amazing how profoundly the encouraging words of just one woman so drastically changed the life of a pitiful, broken teenager who showed up in her driveway one beautiful fall day so many years ago. Her words transformed me into a confident woman with a heart for God."

That's what happens when we believe the best in people…and tell them about it. It can change the course of their lives.

REIGNITING A SMOLDERING FIRE

It is often after a time of apparent failure that a person desperately needs an encouraging word the most. Tell me, hasn't that been the case in your life? It certainly has been in mine. It certainly was for Peter.

You know the story. At the dinner table, on the night before Jesus went to the cross, He had a chat with His friend Peter. He referred to Peter by his pre-disciple-days name—Simon.

> "Simon, Simon, Satan has asked to sift all of you as wheat. But I have prayed for you, Simon, that your faith may not fail. And when you have turned back, strengthen your brothers."
>
> But he replied, "Lord, I am ready to go with you to prison and to death."
>
> Jesus answered, "I tell you, Peter, before the rooster crows today, you will deny three times that you know me" (Luke 22:31-34).

A few hours later, Peter did just that. Denied that he even knew Jesus. Three times. And then the rooster crowed.

And Peter "went outside and wept bitterly" (22:62). He cried and cried and cried.

I've been there. I wonder if you have been too. I've messed up big-time and cried and cried and cried. I've heard that rooster crowing in my own heart as if saying, "I know what you did."

Peter's fire for Jesus went out. Shame doused buckets of regret on the flames, and they went cold.

But three days later, Jesus rose from the dead. The angel at the empty tomb told Mary Magdalene that Jesus had risen. Then he said, "Go, tell his disciples *and Peter*, 'He is going ahead of you into Galilee. There you will see him, just as he told you'" (Mark 16:7). Jesus knew Peter would be struggling with his failure and called him by name to reassure him of His love.

Several days later, Jesus reignited Peter's fire in a more remarkable way. Here's what happened.

Peter gathered a few of his buddies, launched a boat, and went fishing on the Sea of Galilee. After a night of nothing but empty nets, as the sun rose over the horizon, a man called from the shore: "Have you caught any fish?"

"No," Peter answered. "Not a one."

"Throw your net on the right side of the boat and you will find some," the man called out. When they did, they were unable to haul the net in because of the large number of fish.

At that moment, Peter realized it was Jesus. He jumped into the water and swam to the shore where he came face-to-face with grace. Jesus already had a fire burning. After breakfast, Jesus pulled Peter aside to reignite the fire in his heart.

> "Simon son of John, do you love me more than these?"
>
> "Yes, Lord," he said, "you know that I love you."
>
> Jesus said, "Feed my lambs."
>
> Again Jesus said, "Simon son of John, do you love me?"

He answered, "Yes, Lord, you know that I love you."

Jesus said, "Take care of my sheep."

The third time he said to him, "Simon son of John, do you love me?"…

"Lord, you know all things; you know that I love you."

Jesus said, "Feed my sheep" (John 21:15-17).

Jesus removed the shroud of shame hanging from Peter's guilt-weary shoulders and rallied him to get back to the ministry to which he was called—being a fisher of men, not a fisher of fish. Jesus didn't allow Peter's smoldering cinders to die into a pile of ash. I am so thankful Jesus sees our potential among the ruins and chooses to reignite our flame when the harsh winds of life threaten to extinguish our fire in our belly, or the pressures of this world attempt to snuff out our dreams. But here's the kicker: He tells us to do the same for others. Jesus said, "I believe in you, Peter; feed my sheep." We can feed God's sheep as well.

Once there was a young African-American girl with great singing potential. However, she made her debut at New York's Town Hall too early. She wasn't ready, and the critics destroyed her. She returned home to Philadelphia in disgrace. Her church had pooled their meager dimes and nickels for "The Fund for Marian Anderson's Future," and after her apparent failure, she didn't know how she would ever face them again.

For more than a year, Marian's voice went silent under the strains of depression and disgrace. But while her hopes smoldered near extinction, her mother would not allow the dream to die. She continued to use her words to keep the dream alive. "You have a gift," she said. "This failure is only temporary."

Finally, her mother's words began to sink in. "Marian, grace must come before greatness," she said. "Why don't you think about this failure a little and pray about it a lot?"

Marian Anderson, who did go on to become a great vocalist who helped others reach their dreams, said, "Whatever is in my voice, faith put there. Faith and my mother's words: 'Grace must come before greatness.'"[2]

That is the potential of a woman's words. Just as Jesus used His words to reignite Peter's shame-doused passion, we can use our words to reignite the dreams extinguished by life.

UNLOCKING POTENTIAL

Carolyn was a little girl whose dreams were extinguished by the careless words of a very critical teacher. She loved to paint, and when her art teacher asked the class to paint a horse, she painted a picture of a pink-and-purple polka-dotted pony. But rather than praise Carolyn's creativity, she rebuked her for "painting a lie." "There is no such thing as a pink-and-purple polka-dotted pony," she told her. "No talent here."

So, Carolyn decided that no one would ever see her painting again. She only painted the walls in her closet—a place where no one would see. However, one day her mother took some friends up to Carolyn's closet to see a dress she had made for her. When they opened the door, the ladies were surprised to see the walls covered in beautiful art.

"Why, Carolyn," her mother exclaimed. "You're a painter!"

Today, Carolyn Blish is an award-winning member of the American Watercolor Society and Allied Artists of America. Reproductions of her paintings are in fine art galleries, and her prints have received international acclaim.[3] Her book *Drawing Closer* sits on my coffee table today.

Is there someone in your world who has talent hidden away in a closet? Perhaps you hold the key to unlocking their potential and setting it free! Look around. Pay attention. Say the word.

GIVING HOPE TO THE HOPELESS

Sometimes, God will bring people who need encouragement across our paths in the most mysterious ways. That's why we need to slow down and look around. Be sensitive to the little nudges of the Holy Spirit. You never know when you will be someone else's miracle.

Jon Robinson experienced an unexpected miracle at a crucial time in his life. He was a longtime media personality in my hometown, but when he was passed over for an anchor position he thought he had earned, he quit his job at the local television network and sank into a depression. He was hurting and alone. But an unusual twist of fate turned his life around. It all began with a wrong number.

Jon was sitting in the Waterfront Park in Charleston, South Carolina, watching seagulls soaring happily over the pristine harbor. He had taken a job in Charleston, but he missed his son back in Charlotte and mourned that he only got to see him on weekends. He was sinking in his sorrows, pondering the unwanted twists and turns of his life and wondering what his next step should be. Jon wasn't happy with his circumstances and knew he was drinking too much. Something needed to change.

Jon's musings were interrupted by the familiar ring of his cell phone.

He never answered his cell phone unless he knew the caller. He didn't recognize the number, but for some reason he mechanically answered and said, "Hello?"

"I'm sorry," the caller apologized. "I must have the wrong number."

"No problem," Jon replied.

"Well, before I hang up, I want you to know that God loves you, and I'm praying for you," the caller continued.

"You must be out of your mind."

"No. This is a message God wants you to hear."

Jon was intrigued by this woman, and they began talking. Before he knew it, he was spilling out his heart and sharing his personal and professional problems. As he told of his hurt, she shared her hope. He poured out his soul-wrenching misery; she poured in her life-giving message. The caller told Jon about the hope and healing of Jesus Christ, and God began to open his eyes to the possibility of a new life.

For most of his life, Jon had been an agnostic. But since that "wrong number" with the "right answer," Jon has committed his life to Jesus Christ. "I am a Christian. I've had an awakening."[4] That is the power of a woman's words. While we blunder through our days with wrong turns and wrong numbers, we have the right answer! We possess the potential to change the course of a life for all eternity.

POINTING PEOPLE IN
THE RIGHT DIRECTION

I live in Charlotte, North Carolina, 200 miles from the coast. And yet our local Walmart has a random smattering of seagulls that soar overhead and eat french fries and other debris from neighboring fast-food restaurants. The truth is, the seagulls are lost. They've taken a wrong turn. And instead of discovering where they went wrong, they've settled for an asphalt parking lot rather than the salty sea. They've reconciled themselves to feeding on the refuse and trash of harried shoppers rather than the fresh seafood cuisine of their feathered forefathers.

It's not just the seagulls who are lost...who have forgotten the reason for their very existence, the habitat for which they were created to survive and thrive. Many human beings have done the same. Some are lost. They've taken a wrong turn and don't know how to get back to where they need to be. They're standing in the parking lot of life, subsisting off the refuse of fast living.

Someone needs to point them to the ocean of opportunity and the sea of success. And I'm not talking about money or materialism... those things *are* mere french fries compared to the abundant life God has for His children. "'I know the plans I have for you,' declares the LORD, 'plans to prosper you and not to harm you, plans to give you hope and a future'" (Jeremiah 29:11).

Let's hang the fire extinguisher back in the corner and become encouragers who fan even the smallest spark of potential into flame. Many are just waiting for someone who believes in them...and who will tell them so. That someone could be you.

PART TWO

The People
We Impact

4

A BIG Impact on little People

THE POWER OF A WOMAN'S WORDS TO HER CHILDREN

Love your children with all your heart...Praise them for important things...Praise them a lot. They live on it like bread and butter.

LAVINA CHRISTENSEN FUGAL

Now that we know the power of our words, let's look at how they impact different people in our world. First, we're going to start with children, because that's where God starts with us. We're not just talking about how our words affect our own children, but children in general. All through life we will have the opportunity to speak into the little people, and just the right word from you can change a little life forever.

We come into the world as malleable souls who are shaped and molded by the people in our own pint-sized world. And before you know it, we are sitting at the potter's wheel surrounded by little people of our own.

I have often heard that it is better to build children than repair adults, so let's start our journey of discovering the power of a woman's words and the people we impact with those who are most vulnerable... children.

From the time a child emerges from the safety of a mother's womb, he or she is formed and fashioned by the power of a mother's words. With her eyes locked on her new little bundle of squirming love, as she coos, comforts, and coaxes this miraculous gift from God, she truly becomes the mirror in which the child sees himself, whether good or bad.

A mother cheers for her bundle of joy when he rolls over, laughs, and kicks his tiny feet into the air. She even gives a hurrah when her precious angel burps! A mother encourages her babe when he shakes a rattle, holds a cup, points to a color, and responds to his name. But most of all, she lets her child know "I love you just because you're mine."

It is an awesome responsibility, this job called motherhood. We have the privilege of shaping and molding an eternal soul for a very short, very fleeting moment of time. And one of the primary ways we accomplish this feat is with the words we speak.

When we hold that tiny blessing in our arms for the very first time, a flood of hopes and dreams emerges like a great blue whale cresting to spout his spray into the air. But somewhere in the day-to-day busyness of life, encouraging words can get lost among the to-dos and not-to-dos. We need to take a fresh look at motherhood and recapture the commitment to be the great encouragers along a child's journey toward adulthood.

Whether you have children of your own or have the privilege of influencing other people's, you have the ability to impact a child's heart for good or bad. Marion observed the power of *her* mother's words in the life of a little girl who seemed to have lost her way.

MAMA'S PLAN

Marion was entering first grade when she saw the transformation that took place. She loved everything about school: the smell of the chalk and color of the crayons; the way the old wooden floors smelled after Jim, the janitor, had waxed them; having her own desk that was just her size; and her teacher, Miss Edna. She decided that all angels must have blue eyes and smell like Jergen's lotion because that was what

Miss Edna looked and smelled like. The only thing she did not like about first grade was Mildred.

Now, Mildred had already been to first grade one time, and she was bigger than everybody else. She didn't have any friends and seemed to concentrate on making enemies. Because Marion was one of the smallest in the class, Mildred singled her out as her number-one enemy. Each day, as Marion walked home from school in her small town, Mildred taunted her. She came up behind her and stepped on the backs of her shoes, causing them to slide down. Then when Marion stopped to adjust them, Mildred slapped her hard on the back. Marion dreaded the walk home.

Each day, when the school bell rang for dismissal, Marion blinked back the tears that threatened to spill from her fearful eyes. Eventually, Marion's mother figured out something was wrong at school. Marion reluctantly told her mom about Mildred but begged her not to intervene, knowing it would only make it worse.

"You can't do anything, Mama," Marion cried. "You can't. Everyone will think I'm a baby."

Marion's father had died a few years earlier, and her mother worked very hard. It was impossible for her to drive or walk Marion to school, and she didn't have any brothers or sisters to look after her. This was in the days when a little girl walking a few blocks alone to school was nothing unusual, and most of her friends walked or rode their bikes to school as well. But the problem of Mildred weighed heavy on Marion's mom's heart. The following day, Miss Edna asked Marion to stay after school to clean the erasers. Thinking that perhaps Mildred would be long gone by the time she walked home, Marion's heart was relieved. However, when Marion left school, her tormentor was waiting at the top of the hill.

Seeing her daughter in tears yet again, this wise mother came up with a plan. The following day she decided to walk her daughter to school. Marion was nervous about what was going to happen and mortified at her mom's insistence.

"Why couldn't my mother understand that no plan she had dreamed up was going to work?" Marion later recounted. "We bundled up against the bitter cold and started walking up the hill. Maybe we wouldn't see Mildred, I hoped. But my mother had this confident look. I knew the look well, and I had a sinking feeling that we would see Mildred and that Mother would use her 'plan.'

"Sure enough, just as we got to the top of the hill and had to go in one direction to school and my mother in the opposite direction to her job at the bank, we spotted Mildred. We waited a few horrible moments as Mildred approached us. She pretended not to see us when she realized I had my mother with me.

" 'Hello, Mildred,' Mother said quietly. Mildred stopped, frozen as still as a statue. Her hands and face were bright red from the intense cold. Her oversized coat hung open. There were only two buttons on it. The rest were missing. Underneath she wore a cotton dress, as though it were summer. I was wrapped up so snugly, I could hardly walk. I even had to wear undershirts.

"Mother stooped down to Mildred's level. She didn't say anything at first. Instead she rapidly buttoned Mildred's coat and turned up the collar around her neck. Then she fastened back this stubborn piece of hair that forever hung in Mildred's face. I stood off to one side watching our breath linger in front of our faces in the frigid morning air, praying that no students would happen by and that my mother's plan would be over quickly.

" 'I'm Marion's mother. I need your help, Mildred.'

"Mildred looked intently at my mother with an expression I couldn't identify. Their faces were inches apart.

"My mother's gloved hands held Mildred's cold ones as she spoke. 'Marion doesn't have any brothers or sisters. She sort of needs a special best friend at school. Someone to walk up the hill with her after school. You look like you'd be a fine friend for her. Would you be Marion's friend, Mildred?'

"Mildred chewed on her bottom lip, blinking all the time, and then nodded.

" 'Oh, thank you!' Mama said with certain confidence and gratitude. 'I just know you are someone I can depend on.' Then she hugged Mildred long and hard. She gave me a quick hug and called to us as though nothing unusual had happened. 'Bye, girls. Have a good day.' "

Both girls continued walking to school, stiffly, like mechanical dolls staring straight ahead. Once Marion cut her eyes over toward Mildred and saw something she had never seen before…Mildred was smiling.

Time passed, and Marion and Mildred became friends—best friends. As a matter of fact, Mildred starting having lots of friends. She started making good grades, and her desk wasn't so messy anymore. And she always wore her coat collar flipped up and that scraggly piece of hair pinned over to the side, just the way Marion's mom had fixed it. On Valentine's Day, when all the kids cut out cards from red, pink, and white construction paper, Mildred gave Marion a store-bought card and signed it *From Your Best Friend, Mil.*[1]

What was Mama's plan? Her plan was to give encouraging words to a little girl who had been knocked down by life. To tell a floundering child that someone believed in her, trusted her, and entrusted her with her most prized possession. Those words changed the course of Mildred's life.

THE OVERWHELMING WEIGHT OF NEGATIVE WORDS

Studies show that for every negative word spoken, it takes five to seven positive words to balance it out. That means that if a child hears something negative said to him or about him, it takes five to seven positive words to neutralize it. At the same time, studies show that in the average home, ten negative comments are made for every positive one.[2] With that ratio, it's easy to understand why so many children are discouraged and suffer from a poor self-image. Negative language makes children feel discouraged and breeds an environment of low self-esteem.

We can't always see the destructive potential of our words, but let's imagine the following scenario. Your child gets up in the morning and dresses in a shingled outfit much like the Jolly Green Giant on the vegetable labels. The only difference is the outfit is made of Post-it Notes. Every time you question his worth, criticize his work, find fault with his appearance, disapprove of his choices, point out his weakness, or make him feel guilty, the hurtful words are scribbled across a slip of yellow paper, and it flutters to the ground. Perhaps when you see the paper begin to fall, you realize the effect of your hurtful words and try to stick the paper back on with a positive word. However, it won't stick. The sticky has gone right out of it. Then the child goes off to school and hears more discouraging words, and more Post-it Notes fall to the ground. Finally, at the end of the day, the child comes home, exposed, naked, and insecure—and rightly so.

As a mom, we can cover our kids with positive words so that when the negative ones cause a Post-it Note to fall, they won't even know it's missing. But it takes a lot of work.

Paul wrote to the Colossians, "Fathers, do not provoke or irritate or fret your children [do not be hard on them or harass them], lest they become discouraged and sullen and morose and feel inferior and frustrated. [Do not break their spirit.]" (Colossians 3:21 AMPC). Can I add something to Paul's exhortation? Mothers, don't you do it either.

It's a terrible thing to be a part of a family when the only things that are noticed are mistakes. The pain from constant criticism and correction can become a chronic source of insecurity long after the child has become an adult. It is our job as parents to instruct and correct our children, but when we are continually pointing out their faults and failures, they tend to simply stop trying.

We must always remember that children are children, and they will act like children. Children are not miniature adults. I remember when my husband was in dental school at the ripe old age of 23. It was his first time treating a four-year-old little girl, and he was unprepared for the crocodile tears that rolled down her cheeks.

"You'll be fine," Steve assured her with a pat on her shoulder. "You be a big girl now."

Then she looked up at him with big, blue eyes that melted his heart. "But I'm not a big girl," she said. "I'm just a little girl."

That's what we must always remember. No matter how frustrated or angry we become...kids are kids, and they will act like kids.

Here's an idea. Try catching a child doing something right, and then praise him or her for it! "Keesha, I saw the way you helped your brother with his homework! Great job." "Tyler, I noticed how well you cleaned the mud off of your shoes before you came in the house. Thank you." Consider the words to this poem:

TALE OF TWO HOUSEHOLDS

"I got two A's," the small boy said.
His voice was filled with glee.
His father very bluntly asked,
"Why didn't you get three?"
"Mom, I've got the dishes done,"
The girl called from the door.
Her mother very calmly said,
"Did you sweep the floor?"
"I mowed the grass," the tall boy said,
"And put the mower away."
His father asked him with a shrug,
"Did you clean off the clay?"
The children in the house next door
Seemed happy and content.
The same things happened over there,
But this is how it went.
"I got two A's," the small boy said.
His voice was filled with glee.
His father proudly said, "That's great;
I'm glad you belong to me."
"Mom, I got the dishes done,"
The girl called from the door.
Her mother smiled and softly said,
"Each day I love you more."
"I've mowed the grass," the tall boy said.
"And put the mower away."
His father answered with much joy,
"You've made my happy day!"

Children deserve just simple praise
For the tasks they're asked to do.
If they're to lead a happy life,
So much depends on you!

Author Unknown

I remember taking my son, Steven, to an amusement park just before he began fourth grade. It was hot, the lines were long, and I began to feel queasy from being gyrated and jerked to sudden stops from 60 miles per hour. Feeling quite the martyr, I was just about to remind Steven how lucky he was to have a mother like me to bring him to an amusement park. But before the words escaped from my mouth, the Holy Spirit gently stopped me. Was that what I really wanted to say? Would those words make Steven feel "lucky," or would they make him feel guilty, as though he owed me something?

Instead of saying my initial thought, I wrapped my arms around my precious young son and said, "Steven, I am so lucky to have a son like you that I can bring to an amusement park." With those words, a dimpled smile spread across his precious face, and I was thankful for the splash of the watery roller coaster that disguised the tears streaming down my face.

If I had spoken that first sentence, Steven would not have felt lucky to have a mom like me at all. He would have felt guilty and that he needed to pay me back for my "kindness." However, the revised version made him feel special, treasured, and loved.

Now, who was encouraged? Actually, we both were.

Perhaps you have some old tapes from your past that you tend to replay with your children. Did your mother make comments that caused you to feel guilty or as if you were indebted to her for the care she gave you? Perhaps she still does. Many moms could be travel agents for guilt trips. Is that how you want to be remembered?

Making our kids feel guilty is like causing emotional heartburn. It just keeps on coming back and coming back. But, Mom, we can change the verbal menu and decide to serve up a dish of words that don't cause indigestion!

I had success with my words that day at the amusement park, but not every day has been a banner day. I have used my words to tear down instead of build up. I have failed many times. "The tongue is a fire, the very world of iniquity," as James so aptly points out (James 3:6 NASB). It can only be tamed by the power of the Holy Spirit, prayer, and practice. Just like a wild lion who is trained by hours and hours of discipline, so our tongue can be tamed to behave. We will get into more about how to tame this wild beast in a later chapter.

> It is our job as parents to instruct and correct our children, but when we are continually pointing out their faults and failures, they tend to simply stop trying.

THE CHOICE TO BECOME A CHIEF CHEERLEADER OR CHIEF CRITIC

Every day we have a choice. Will we build up our children or tear them down? Will we speak words of life or of death? Are we a child's chief cheerleader or chief critic?

William Barclay tells a story of a mom who made a choice to speak words of life. One day Benjamin West's mother went out to run a few errands, leaving him in charge of his little sister, Sally. In his mother's absence, he discovered some bottles of colored ink, and to amuse Sally, he began to paint her portrait. In doing so, he made quite a mess of things...spilling numerous ink splotches here and there. When his mother returned, she saw the mess but said nothing about it. Instead, she deliberately looked beyond the spilt ink as she picked up the piece of paper. Smiling, she exclaimed, "Why, it's Sally!" She then stooped and kissed her son. From that time on, Benjamin West would say, "My mother's kiss made me a painter."[3]

I'm not sure that would have been my initial response, but what an inspiration Benjamin's mom is to me. Could it be that so many kids abandon their dreams because they hear more about their messes than their masterpieces?

Cheers really do make a difference. My son ran cross-country in high school. On the way to one of Steven's races, I got lost, which for anyone who knows me is no surprise. I was so thankful he had ridden the bus with the team. The races only lasted about 20 minutes, so it was important to be on time. I arrived just as the runners were walking off the trail, having missed the race altogether.

On the way home, Steven said, "You know, there were so many parents and fans cheering for the other teams and hardly anybody yelling for us. When I ran by and heard them cheering for their kids, it actually made me go slower. I didn't think it would really matter that much, but it did."

Researcher Tim Rees reported that "ongoing support of friends and family may be one of the most important factors influencing sports performance. He believes that the encouragement and support of friends and family is a key factor in building confidence in an athlete, and it's this confidence that can lead to success in a high-pressure sporting event."[4]

If we leave our child's cheering section—if our seat is vacant—the child will look for someone else to fill it. That someone is usually a peer who may have issues of their own. A child begins to try to please whoever is occupying that seat in the stands. So dust off those pom-poms! Ready that megaphone! Be about the business of becoming your child's greatest fan!

Could it be that so many kids abandon their dreams because they hear more about their messes than their masterpieces?

My nephew Stu also ran cross-country. He began running on his school team when he was in the eighth grade. Since we lived 200 miles from his home, I didn't get to watch him compete. However, I heard the main attraction at Stu's races was not the runners, but his enthusiastic mother.

Finally, when Stu was a senior in high school, his team came to my hometown for a state meet. I don't know if you have ever been to a cross-country race, but it is not exactly a spectator sport. Runners line up on the starting mark. A man fires a starting gun for the race to begin. Then the participants disappear down a trail in the woods, only to reappear some 16 minutes later.

Before the race, my family and I stood on the sidelines, watching legs stretch, backs bend, and arms swing in an effort to warm up. Seventy anxious young men clustered around the starting line in ready position. The shot fired into the air, and the herd of boys began their 3.1-mile run through the woods. As soon as Stu's foot left the starting position, his mother, Pat, picked up her 36-inch megaphone and began to yell louder than any woman I have ever heard.

"GO, STU!" she cheered, not once but at ten-second intervals. When he was out of sight, she ran to another strategic spot along the winding trail where the runners would eventually pass by. And even though the boys were nowhere in sight, Pat continued to cheer, "GO, STU!"

"Pat, do you have to yell so loud?" my husband, Steve, asked.

"Yep," she answered. "GO, STU!"

Steve inched his way a few paces behind us and pretended like he had no idea who we were.

"GO, STU!"

I'll admit, it was a little embarrassing. She had no shame.

At one point she yelled, "GO, STU!" and a man in the crowd yelled, "HE CAN'T HEEEAAARRR YOOOUUU!"

"Pat, Stu can't hear you when he's deep in the woods. Why don't you let up a bit?" I asked.

"I don't know if he can hear me or not, but if there's a chance that he can, I want him to hear my voice cheering him on," she answered. So for 16 minutes, this little dynamo continued to pump confidence and inspiration into her son's heart.

After the race, I asked my nephew, "Stu, when you are running on that trail in the woods, can you hear your mother cheering for you?"

"Oh yes," he answered. "I can hear her the whole way."

"And what does that do for you?" I asked.

"It makes me not want to quit," he replied. "When my legs ache and lungs burn, when I feel like I'm going to throw up, I hear my mom's voice cheering for me, and it makes me not want to stop."

A few years later, when my son became a cross-country runner, I learned a few facts about a foot race. As you near the end of a race, your throat burns, your legs ache, and your whole body cries out for you to stop. That's when friends and fans are the most valuable. Their encouragement helps you push through the pain to the finish. That's the power of a mother's words.

A mother's support means a great deal to her children. She is an encourager, whose voice can be heard echoing in the distance, pumping courage and confidence into her children's hearts. She's the cheerleader on the sidelines who knows that an uplifting word, offered at the right moment, might make the difference between her children finishing well or collapsing along the way.

THE UNIQUELY
CREATED MASTERPIECE

Every child wants to know that he or she is unique and special—unlike any other child ever created. Most teens think they are different, but not in a good way. They see themselves as not as pretty, smart, athletic, popular, funny, and cool as other teens. Adolescents tend to see themselves through the critical lens of pop culture and social media. Instagram, Twitter, Facebook, Snapchat, and so many more to come hold up unrealistic expectations that tell kids they're just not as cool as their peers. Never mind that the Twitter photo took 20 tries to get one that was post-able. We live in a culture of comparison that constantly tells kids they're not enough. And I'm not talking about just teens and adolescents. The average age for getting a first phone is just ten years old, and half of all twelve-year-olds have social media accounts.[5]

But just suppose a child has a mother or a person of influence who has explained about his uniqueness. Just suppose a child has someone speaking into her life who reminds her of God's distinctive design and plan for her life…that she possesses features and talents that were created in her for a specific, God-ordained purpose. I wonder if the words would serve as a defense for the insecurities that tend to knock young adolescents around in the boxing ring of the social melee.

God puts gifts and talents in each child, and it's the parents and adults of influence who help them discover the treasure hidden beneath the freckled face, tousled hair, and muddy feet. A wise woman looks beyond pink hair bows, pouty lips, and rosy cheeks. By being specific with our praise, a child believes what you perceive. Again, you become the mirror from which your child sees herself.

My friend Glynnis has five children. She and her husband are experts at discovering the uniqueness of each one. They study, observe, listen, and ponder these fascinating creatures, and then help them recognize their distinctive gifts. Here are her words of wisdom for us.

Having three boys, who by nature are competitive, challenged me to be creative in how I encouraged their individual strengths. When they started comparing themselves to each other in athletics and academics, they began to focus on their own personal weaknesses. One thing we did to help them see their strengths was to compare each one to an animal that shared a similar characteristic. Josh is solid and strong, and he became our lion. Robbie is thin and nimble, and he became our cheetah. Dylan is fast and savvy, and he was our jaguar. The boys loved being compared to a beautiful animal, and they caught a glimpse of their unique abilities.

When I was a little girl, my dad used to count my freckles with pleasure. As a result, I grew up liking my freckles. To help my boys feel better about their physical features,

I've always told them how much I enjoy very specific parts of their makeup. "I love your brown eyes," I'd say. "They remind me of chocolate, and you know how much I love chocolate!" "Dylan, I love your wavy hair," I'd muse. "It reminds me of the ocean." "Robbie, I love your straight hair," I'd remark. "It shines just like gold when the sun shines on it."

Now that we have adopted two little girls from Africa, I am finding new challenges to help them see their uniqueness. The younger girl, Ruth, immediately started talking about how much she loved our white skin and how she wished she were white. "But look how the sun glistens on your beautiful brown skin when I put lotion on it," I said. Pretty soon her smile and attitude matched the glow of her beautiful brown skin. It has been months since she has mentioned her skin, and she loves to put lotion on it.

Most of all, I have taught each of my kids to be the best at who God made them to be. "Joshua," I'd say, "be the best Joshua you can be." "Dylan, be the best Dylan you can be." "Robbie, be the best Robbie you can be." "Ruth, be the best Ruth you can be." "Cathrine, be the best Cathrine you can be." It is a joy to watch each one of my children blooming into the confident young men and women God wants them to be. Thankfully, they don't try to be anyone else.

By being specific with our praise, a child believes what you perceive.

God has specific plans for each human being. While a mother doesn't know what those specific plans are for her children, she can give them the tools of discovery, point them to the treasure map, and help them see the clues along the way.

A mother's words can be the breeze that fills the sails of a child's hopes and dreams to propel them to new horizons. However, we must be careful that the wind that fills their sails sends them in the direction God has planned and the direction we would like for them to take. Did you notice how specific Glynnis was in her praise? "Great job," "You're terrific," and "Way to go!" are all wonderful pats on the back. However, being specific with praise is more powerful and makes a greater impact. "I couldn't believe how far you hit that baseball. Man, you've got an incredible swing." "That cartwheel was amazing. Your legs stuck up straight in the air just like a professional gymnast." "I noticed the way you helped Mary with her homework. You have such a generous heart. I want to be more like you."

Do you see the difference? Being specific moves encouraging words from good to great.

A great mom will discover a child's gifts and talents and then use her words to fertilize that gift. She will help them realize the words of the psalmist, "I praise you because I am fearfully and wonderfully made" (Psalm 139:14), are meant specifically for them. If a child becomes good at one thing, he or she will believe that success is achievable in other areas of life as well and won't be afraid to attempt them. We don't have to be a millionaire to let our children know they are rich. Encouraging words are free for the giving with bountiful results.

Thomas Edison, one of America's greatest inventors, had this to say about the positive influence of his mother's words on his own life:

> I did not have my mother long, but she cast over me an influence which has lasted all my life. The good effect of her early training I can never lose. If it had not been for her appreciation and her faith in me at a critical time in my experience, I should never likely have become an inventor. I was always a careless boy, and with a mother of different mental caliber, I should have turned out badly. But her firmness, her sweetness, her goodness were potent powers to keep me on the right path. My mother was the making of me.[6]

While we do want to discover the uniqueness of each child, our praise must consist of verbal applause for more than appearance and talents. The most important traits we praise are those that exhibit godly character. The Bible calls these "the fruit of the Spirit": love, joy, peace, patience, kindness, goodness, faithfulness, gentleness, and self-control (Galatians 5:22-23). If even a sprout of these fruits peeks through the soil, a wise mother will fertilize the sprout with positive words in hopes of a bountiful harvest.

THE POWER OF BELIEVING THE BEST

Sometimes all a child needs is for someone to believe the best in him, rather than the worst. That someone could be a parent, a teacher, a coach, or a neighbor. Howard Hendricks saw how one simple comment by a wise teacher changed the entire course of his life.

By the fifth grade, Howard was bearing all the fruit of a kid who felt insecure, unloved, and angry at life. In other words, he was tearing the place apart. However, his teacher, Miss Simon, apparently thought he was blind to this problem because she regularly reminded him, "Howard, you are the worst-behaved child in this school!"

So tell me something I don't already know! he thought to himself as he proceeded to live up (or down) to her opinion of him. I'll let Dr. Hendricks tell you the rest of the story.

> Needless to say, the fifth grade was probably the worst year of my life. Finally I graduated—for obvious reasons. But I left with Miss Simon's words ringing in my ears: "Howard, you are the worst-behaved child in this school!"
>
> You can imagine what my expectations were upon entering the sixth grade. The first day of class, my teacher Miss Noe went down the roll call, and it wasn't long before she came to my name. "Howard Hendricks," she called out, glancing from her list to where I was sitting with my arms folded, just waiting to go into action. She looked me over for a moment and then said, "I've heard a lot about you." Then she smiled and added, "But I don't believe a word of it!"

I tell you, that moment was a fundamental turning point, not only in my education, but in my life. Suddenly, unexpectedly, someone believed in me. For the first time in my life, someone saw potential in me. Miss Noe put me on special assignments. She gave me little jobs to do. She invited me to come in after school to work on my reading and arithmetic. She challenged me with higher standards.

I had a hard time letting her down…

What made the difference between fifth grade and sixth? The fact that someone was willing to give me a chance. Someone was willing to believe in me while challenging me with higher expectations.[7]

Many times a child doesn't act capable because he is treated as though he's not. Goethe said, "Treat a man as he appears to be, and you make him worse. But treat a man as if he already were what he potentially could be, and you make him what he should be." Howard Hendricks experienced the power of a woman's words to change the course of his life. He went on to become a longtime professor at Dallas Theological Seminary. I wonder how many men and women Dr. Hendricks gave a chance—believed in and challenged with high expectations?

I saw this happen with my own son when he was in the seventh grade. He was taking advanced math, advanced English, advanced science, and Latin. It was also his first year playing on a school sports team, and he got home about 6:00 at night. Nothing was going well. It was hard to get his schoolwork done when he came home exhausted. A few times he had worked hard on an assignment, only to find that he had done the wrong page. Latin was Greek to him, and there was no sign that he was going to catch on anytime soon.

One day after practice, I heard him in the shower crying out to God. "Lord, I'm not good at anything. Just help me be good at something. Just one thing."

That broke my heart. Actually, Steven was great at many things, but his emotions and workload were too much to bear. I met with the principal, and we dropped one of the advanced courses (Latin), but his year really turned around with a written note from one of his teachers, who knew he was struggling and needed an extra pat on the back. In it she wrote:

> *Dear Mr. and Mrs. Jaynes,*
>
> *Steven has been doing excellent work in science. His name has been at the top of the list on recent tests and quizzes. No doubt he told you about his perfect score on our last test. He is a fine young man. I would love a room full of Stevens!*
>
> *Best regards,*
> *Mrs. Connie Roads*

Though this note of encouragement was addressed to Steven's dad and me, in reality it was for our son. Mrs. Roads is a very wise woman who looked past the tough exterior of adolescence and saw a tender, hurting heart. It was the turning point of our son's year. She gave Steven the encouragement he needed in her written words, and he was ready to stay the course and finish well.

Oh, friend, we have so much power in our words. Whether they are spoken through the lips of a wise woman or penned by the hand of a willing writer, our words can change the course of a life.

THE LEGACY WE LEAVE BEHIND

Each day hundreds of people ferry across New York Harbor to view the Statue of Liberty, who has welcomed weary travelers to the American shore. Lady Liberty was a gift of friendship from the people of France in 1886 and has stood as a symbol of freedom for thousands who have escaped the tyranny and poverty of distant lands. With torch held high, she proclaims, "Give me your tired, your poor, your huddled masses yearning to breathe free."

And who did the famous sculptor use to model the face of inspiration for this beacon of freedom and faith? His mother. Frederic Bartholdi chose his own mother's face as the model for the Statue of Liberty to represent freedom and faith to all who enter the United States via New York Harbor. Like a stately lighthouse that guides seafaring ships safely to shore, mothers stand as sentinels on the rough shoreline of life to guide their tiny fleet safely home and back out to sea.

When our children grow to maturity, whom will they think of when they reflect on their own heritage of freedom and faith? What will be our legacy of words? Oh, dear friend, I hope they, like Frederic Bartholdi, think of their moms, who held high the light of Jesus Christ and gave them roots to keep them grounded and wings to soar.

FUN IDEAS TO ENCOURAGE A CHILD

- Put notes in a lunchbox.
- Write a note on the bathroom mirror with soap.
- Put a note on a pillow.
- Tie a note around a favorite stuffed animal.
- Tuck a note in a textbook.
- Send an e-mail.
- Send a text.
- Post about them on Facebook and tag them.
- Mail them a card.
- Celebrate with a "You Are Special" plate.
- Make a list of 25 reasons you're glad she's your kid.
- Write Scripture prayers for him.
- Point out biblical character traits you see in her.

POWER-PACKED WORDS
Words that Crush a Child's Heart

- You should…
- You ought…
- You can't do anything right.
- You are driving me crazy!
- You make me so upset!
- You make me so angry!
- Why did you do that?
- Why can't you make good grades like your sister/brother?
- Why can't you be sweet like your sister/brother?
- You are a liar. (Change to "You told a lie.")
- You are a thief. (Change to "You stole something.")
- Look at all I've done for you.
- You don't love me.
- You don't appreciate me.
- I've told you a thousand times.
- You'll never learn, will you?
- What's wrong with you?

Simply put, avoid sarcasm, teasing, and subtle put-downs and jokes at a child's expense. If you have to add "I was just kidding" to any statement made to a child, it will most likely wound the child and not be funny at all.

Words a Child Longs to Hear
(There are 50)

- Great job!
- I'm glad you're my son/daughter.
- I love spending time with you.
- I'll never forget the day you were born. You were such an incredible gift from God…and you still are.
- I like you!
- That was really great!
- You're fantastic.
- I love the way you fixed your hair!
- Good thinking!
- You give the best hugs!
- You are so brave!
- You're a great person!
- You've got a great sense of humor.
- You have such a big heart!
- That shirt looks great on you!
- You played that song beautifully!
- You are a great friend!
- You'll make a wonderful wife/husband some day!
- Thanks for cleaning your room. You did a great job.
- You teach me so much about life.
- You're so strong!
- I can always count on you.
- I trust you.
- You are God's special gift to me.

- You light up my day.
- My favorite part of the day is picking you up from school.
- I missed having you around today.
- You're such a good helper.
- I'm so proud of you!
- Way to go!
- I knew you could do it!
- God made a masterpiece when He made you.
- You are such a treasure!
- You are one of God's greatest gifts to me.
- I'm behind you.
- I'm praying for you.
- That was so responsible.
- You're a joy.
- How did you get so smart?
- That was so creative.
- Hurray for you!
- I appreciate you!
- Wow! Look at those muscles!
- You bring other people so much joy.
- You are so thoughtful!
- Thank you for being such a hard worker!
- God went all out when He created you!
- Great idea!
- How did I get the best kid in the world?
- Thank you.

The Dripping Faucet or the Refreshing Well

THE POWER OF A WOMAN'S WORDS TO HER HUSBAND

I like not only to be loved, but also to be told that I am loved.

GEORGE ELIOT

For 13 years our family was blessed with a golden retriever named Ginger. We gave her to our son, Steven, for Christmas when he was five years old, and she still holds the blue ribbon as the best present ever. I can still remember the look of surprise on Steven's little-boy face when the "stuffed" animal began to move. "It's a puppy!" he exclaimed. "It's not a toy!"

And while Ginger was officially Steven's dog, and I was unofficially her primary caretaker, it was my husband, Steve, who held a special place in her heart. From the very beginning, Ginger loved Steve the best.

Ginger lollygagged her days away by sleeping in a sunny place on the driveway or lounging by the back steps. However, when my husband's car entered the neighborhood and turned the corner onto our street, Ginger's ears perked up and her eyes lit up. Suddenly infused with a burst of anticipatory energy, she would jump to her feet and run in circles. "He's home! He's home!" she seemed to say.

When Steve pulled into the garage and opened his car door, Ginger ran to greet him and rested her head on his left leg while he cooed and rubbed her ears. Steve's homecoming was the highlight of her day.

No wonder dog is called "man's best friend." Ginger was loyal, didn't nag, and loved Steve no matter how much or how little attention he paid to her on any given day. She was very forgiving and immediately forgot any injustice, such as withholding her dinner when we ate in her presence or being left behind when we traveled on vacation. Often at the mere sight of Steve, Ginger rolled over on her back and beckoned him to rub her tummy. She always responded to his touch as though it were heaven on earth. What man wouldn't love such a response from "his girl"?

And yet, when God created Adam and placed him in the Garden, only to determine that "it is not good for the man to be alone" (Genesis 2:18), He did not create a dog to be his loyal companion. God created a woman—a woman with words. She was called an *ezer* in the Hebrew— the original language of the Old Testament. Most Bible translations render the word *ezer* as "helper," but the word is packed with so much more meaning than a mere helper.

> *Ezer* appears twenty-one times in the Old Testament. Twice, in Genesis, it describes the woman (Genesis 2:18,20). But the majority of references (sixteen to be exact) refer to God, or Yahweh, as the helper of his people. The remaining three references appear in the books of the prophets, who use it to refer to military aid.[1]

We would be remiss if we looked at the word *ezer* or "helper" as someone who just worked around the house. Adam didn't need someone to cook for him, clean up after him, or care for him. There were no groceries to buy, loads of laundry to wash, or floors to sweep. That was not his problem. The void in Adam's life was that he didn't have a companion to work with him, rule the earth with him, love with him, procreate with him, and—after the fall—struggle with him. A dog might have been an easier adjustment for Adam, but God decided Adam needed someone with words.

"Then God said, 'Let Us make man in Our image'…God created man in His own image, in the image of God He created him; male and female He created them" (Genesis 1:26-27 NASB). All through the Bible we see the word *man* used to refer to "mankind." As in this rendering of the Hebrew word, *man* does not mean "male." Just as a puppy is the offspring of a dog, the word *man* means offspring of a "hu-man." I point this out because many of the verses that we will examine in this book will use the word *man,* but they pertain to women as well.

I saw a placard recently that read, "I always have the last word with my wife. It's 'Yes, dear.'" We chuckle—but it's not really funny, is it? Perhaps "Yes, dear" are the very words Adam said to Eve when she handed him the forbidden fruit.

We looked at James 3:3-6 in chapter 2. Not to change the Word of God by any means, but simply applying it to marriage, we can paraphrase the passage as follows:

"When we put bits into the mouths of horses to make them obey us, we can turn the whole animal." *Likewise, we can change the course of our marriage, one way toward harmony and the other way to discord. Just a tug on the reins of the tongue will do it.*

"Or take ships as an example. Although they are so large and are driven by strong winds, they are steered by a very small rudder wherever the pilot wants to go." *In the same way, winds of responsibility and everyday life drive marriages through the mundane course of life, but one little word from a wife can steer her marriage toward calm seas of love and respect, or toward turbulent waters of anger and bitter resentment.*

"Likewise, the tongue is a small part of the body, but it makes great boasts." *Yes, the tongue is a small part of the body; you wouldn't think it has so much power to affect a marriage. It talks a big talk. Makes big promises. We take solemn vows on our wedding day to love, honor, and obey, but what happens after the honeymoon is often quite different.*

"Consider what a great forest is set on fire by a small spark." *Consider how many marriages go up in flames because of careless and thoughtless words; how many marriages are destroyed because someone refused to filter spoken words through the sieve of kindness.*

"The tongue also is a fire, a world of evil among the parts of the body."

There's nothing worse on a marriage than ill-spoken words. Hurtful behavior can be forgiven and forgotten, but hateful words linger longer.

"It corrupts the whole person, sets the whole course of one's life on fire, and is itself set on fire by hell." *Yes, words are powerful. They can make a marriage heaven or hell on earth.*

Just as wildfires start as a single spark, marriages are destroyed with the tiny spark of an ill-spoken word.

I grew up in a very negative home. Let me preface that with this: I became a Christian when I was 14 years old. My mother came to Christ three years after I did. My dad became a Christ follower three years after my mom. In the years that followed their conversion, much forgiveness and redemption took place.

But during my growing-up years, I was immersed in negative talk. My parents used their words as weapons to try to destroy each other. And unfortunately, they turned those same weapons on their children. Caustic words became a way of life. So I know what it is like to live in an atmosphere of violent arguing, passive-aggressive silence, searing sarcasm, constant criticism, and belittling brawling. I still have the scars to prove it.

When I became a wife, I did not want to repeat the patterns that I learned as a child, but it's not been as simple as making a decision. Changing the words in my head before they escape my lips has taken prayer and practice.

As an *ezer* or a strong helper, how will we use our words? Will we use them to defend or defeat, complete or compete, praise or put down? The choice begins in our minds, runs through our hearts, and responds with our lips. Let's look at a few biblical and modern-day examples of the power of a woman's words on the men in their lives.

WORDS CAN BREAK A MAN

Samson was God's chosen man during a time when the judges ruled Israel. From birth, he was destined to liberate Israel from the taunting Philistines. While Samson was incredibly strong in body, he was very weak in character. Among his character flaws was a weakness for women, especially Philistine women. In his early years, he saw a Philistine woman, liked the Philistine woman, and decided he had to have the Philistine woman. Regardless of his parents' warnings, he married the young vixen, and she slowly but surely used her words to lead him astray.

It all began when Samson was talking to some of the fellows at the wedding party. " 'Let me tell you a riddle,' Samson said to them. 'If you can give me the answer within the seven days of the feast, I will give you thirty linen garments and thirty sets of clothes. If you can't tell me the answer, you must give me thirty linen garments and thirty sets of clothes.'

" 'Tell us your riddle,' they said. 'Let's hear it.'

"He replied, 'Out of the eater, something to eat; out of the strong, something sweet'" (Judges 14:12-14).

The men were perplexed at the riddle and were in fear of losing the shirts off their backs, so they convinced Samson's bride to coax the answer out of him. She whined. She cried. She manipulated. He weakened. He waned. He capitulated. Samson revealed the answer to the riddle to his new wife, and she in turn told her friends. The Philistines kept their shirts, and Samson lost his. As Samson stormed away in a rage, his father handed the bride over to one of his attendants as a parting gift.

Twenty years later, the power of a woman's ill-spoken words had diminished in Samson's memory, and he fell in love with yet another Philistine woman, Delilah. The Philistines saw Samson's infatuation with one of their own as a pathway to discovering the secret to his supernatural strength.

Each of the Philistine officials offered Delilah 1,100 shekels of silver to uncover the secret to his supernatural strength. "See if you can lure him into showing you the secret of his great strength and how we can overpower him so we may tie him up and subdue him" (Judges 16:5). Three times she begged him to tell her the secret source of his strength, and three times he led her astray. But the fourth time she whined. She cried. She manipulated. He weakened. He waned. He capitulated.

Listen to her words and imagine the tone: "How can you say *I love*

you when you won't confide in me? This is the third time you have
made a fool of me and haven't told me the secret of your great strength."
Did you hear the whiny voice? Did it sound just a little familiar? My
toes are hurting.

Then comes the verse that makes me stop in my tracks. "With such
nagging she prodded him day after day until he was sick to death of it"
(Judges 16:15-16). Deep breath. Ouch and double ouch.

Unfortunately, Samson told Delilah the secret of his strength. He
couldn't take the nagging any longer.

"'No razor has ever been used on my head,' he said, 'because I have
been a Nazirite dedicated to God from my mother's womb. If my head
were shaved, my strength would leave me, and I would become as weak
as any other man'" (Judges 16:17).

After Samson divulged the secret to his strength, Delilah lured him
to put his head in her lap, cooed him to sleep, and called for the enemies to come and shave his head. Samson's strength seeped out with
each swipe of the blade. He was bound, blinded, and spent the rest of
his days in bondage...because he succumbed to the power of a woman's ill-spoken words.

Oh, the power of a woman's words on a man who loves her. This
is not the only example of a woman in the Bible who used her words
to bring harm to her husband. Sarai used her words to convince her
husband, Abram, to sleep with her servant girl rather than wait on
God's promise to provide an heir through her. Her words resulted in
the birth of Ishmael and the resulting conflict between the Arab and
Jewish nations that still rages today. Eve used her words to convince
her husband, Adam, to eat the forbidden fruit. Her words resulted in
sin, condemnation, and spiritual death to every man and woman born
under the curse.

Now, before you grow discouraged at examples of how women used
their words in destructive ways, let me give you a bit of hope. Just as
sin was ushered into the world through the words of Eve, salvation and
hope were ushered into the world through the words of Mary. When
the angel Gabriel came to the young teenage virgin and announced
that she would conceive a child by the Holy Spirit, she replied, "Behold,

the bondslave of the Lord; may it be done to me according to your word" (Luke 1:38 NASB). She embraced God's will for her life and used her words to glorify Him in one of the most beautiful songs of praise recorded in the Bible (see Luke 1:46-55). Three cheers for Mary!

WORDS CAN DEBILITATE A MAN

My friend Nancy, like Delilah, used her words to manipulate and debilitate her husband. However, she didn't see the damage it was doing until she heard her words coming out of someone else's mouth. Let's let Nancy tell the story in her own powerful words:

> My brother Dan said, "I'm going home! Your bickering is driving me nuts. Your constant fighting's more irritating than chewing on tinfoil!"
>
> I defended our behavior. "Hey, it's not like we disagree about *everything*. Ron and I agree on all the major issues. We hardly ever fight about 'big stuff,' like how to spend our money, how to raise Nick, or who's a better driver (me). It's just the little stuff that gets to us."
>
> He sighed and said, "Well, I'm sick of hearing you go to war over where to put the towel rack, which TV shows to watch, or who left the lights on. It's all dumb stuff. None of it will matter a year from now. Why did you have to criticize the way he mowed the lawn? I know it wasn't perfect, but couldn't you just let it go?"
>
> "No," I replied. "We are having company tomorrow, and I want the yard to be perfect. So I told him to fix it. Big deal! We were married in the seventies, and Helen Reddy told me that I had to roar if I wanted to be heard, so I roar—and it works, because he re-mowed the lawn and I won."
>
> Dan paused, shook his head, and said, "If you keep this up, you may win the arguments but lose your husband."
>
> I smacked him on the arm and said, "Oh, stop being so melodramatic!"

The next evening Ron and I went out to dinner with some friends we hadn't seen in several years. We remembered Carl as being funny and outgoing, but he seemed rather sad and looked exhausted. His wife, Beth, did most of the talking. She told us about her fabulous accomplishments at work and then endlessly bragged about her brilliant, college-bound children.

She didn't mention her husband except to criticize him.

After we ordered our dinner, she said, "Carl, I saw you flirting with that waitress!" (He wasn't.)

"Caarrrrlll," she whined a little while later, "can't you do anything right? You are holding your fork like a little kid!" (He was.)

When he mispronounced an item on the dessert menu, his wife said, "No wonder you flunked out of college. You can't read!" She laughed so hard she snorted, but she was the only one laughing.

Carl didn't respond. He just looked over at us with an empty face and a blank stare. Then he shrugged his sad shoulders and looked away.

The rest of the evening was even more oppressive as she continued to harangue and harass him about almost everything he said or did. I thought, *I wonder if this is how my brother feels when I criticize Ron.*

We said goodbye to Beth and Carl and left the restaurant in silence. When we got in the car, I spoke first. "Do I sound like her?"

Ron said, "You're not *that* bad."

I asked, "How bad am I?"

"Pretty bad," he half whispered.

The next morning, as I poured water into the coffeepot, I looked over at my "Famous Quotes for Wives" calendar.

"The wise woman builds her house, but the foolish tears it down with her own hands." *Or with her own mouth,* I thought.

"A nagging wife annoys like a constant dripping." *How did I turn into such a nag?*

"Put a guard over my mouth." *Oh, Lord, show me how!*

As I carefully spooned the vanilla nut decaf into the pot, I remembered the day I forgot the filter. The coffee was bitter and full of undrinkable grounds. I had to throw it away.

Then it dawned on me. *The coffee, without filtering, is like my coarse and bitter speech.*

I said, "Oh, God, please install a filter between my brain and my mouth. Help me to choose my words carefully and speak in smooth and mellow tones. Thank You for teaching me the lesson of the coffee filter. I won't forget it."

An hour later, Ron timidly asked, "What do you think about moving the couch over by the window? We'll be able to see the TV better."

My first thought was, *That's a dumb idea! The couch will fade if you put it in the sunlight, and besides, you already watch too much TV.*

But instead of my usual hasty reply, I let the coarse thoughts drip through my newly installed filter and smiled as I said, "That might be a good idea. Let's try it for a few days and see if we like it. I'll help you move it!"

He lifted his end of the sofa in stunned silence. Once we had it in place, he asked with concern, "Are you okay? Do you have a headache?"

I chuckled. "I'm great, honey. Never better. Can I get you a cup of coffee?"

Ron and I recently celebrated our twenty-seventh wedding anniversary, and I'm happy to report that my "filter" is still in place—although it occasionally springs a leak! I've also expanded the filter principle beyond my marriage, and I have found it amazingly useful when I speak to telemarketers, traffic cops, and teenagers.[2]

When Nancy heard her words coming out of someone else's mouth, she was appalled and ashamed. Maybe you've felt the same way at times. But, thank God, we can listen, learn, and make a decision to leave the critical spirit behind and put the filter of grace securely in place.

WORDS CAN MAKE A MAN

Billy Graham was one of the greatest evangelists and Christian leaders of our time. His lifelong mission of giving hope through a relationship with Jesus Christ led him to preach to live audiences totaling 210 million people in more than 185 countries. As of 2008, his estimated lifetime audience, including radio and television, topped 2.2 billion. What began in a one-room office in Minneapolis, Minnesota, in 1950, grew to become the Billy Graham Evangelistic Association and has taken the gospel to the farthest corners of the globe. And while Mr. Graham has been celebrated by presidents, the press, and millions of people for his passion to preach the gospel, he was quick to say that it was his wife, Ruth, who deserved the praise.

"Ruth and I were called by God as a team," he said. "She urged me to go, saying 'God has given you the gift of an evangelist. I'll back you. I'll rear the children, and you travel and preach'...I'd come home and she had everything so organized and so calmed down that they all seemed to love me. But that was because she taught them to."[3]

Yes, it was Billy Graham's face the multitudes watched and his fiery sermons they watched, but it was Ruth, his wife, who gave him the courage and strength to disappear down their long driveway and leave home to do what God had called him to do.

"They [the children] were mighty good about him being gone so much because they knew why he was gone," Ruth remembered.[4] And how did they gain that deep understanding of why Daddy was gone?

Because of the power of one woman's words to instill the passion of the gospel and the urgency of the message that their father preached.

"Without Ruth's partnership and encouragement over the years, my own work would have been impossible," Mr. Graham said.

On June 14, 2007, Ruth Bell Graham, this amazing woman of God who used her words to give strength and courage to a farm boy from Charlotte, North Carolina, went home to be with God. At her funeral, Billy Graham stood up to thank God for the precious gift of Ruth. "My wife, Ruth, was the most incredible woman I have ever known," he said. "Whenever I was asked to name the finest Christian I ever met, I always replied, 'My wife, Ruth.' She was a spiritual giant whose unparalleled knowledge of the Bible and commitment to prayer were a challenge and inspiration to everyone who knew her."[5]

That is the power of a woman's words to make her man...to help him be all that God intended.

My dictionary defines *encouragement* as "the act of inspiring others with renewed courage, renewed spirit, or renewed hope." That beautifully describes the power of Ruth Graham toward her husband.

"Yes, love believes all things. It sticks up for seemingly impossible dreams, cheering as those dreams struggle forward and applauding when they finally come true."[6] Just as Delilah used her words to break her man, Ruth used her words to make her man. And we can too.

WORDS CAN DEVASTATE A MAN

Perhaps you are holding this book with a heavy heart because you know that the words that you speak to your husband have not been loving, kind, encouraging, or supportive. Perhaps you've forgotten the thrill of the early years when he walked into a room, the melting warmth when he called on the phone, or the exhilarating joy of becoming one when body and soul united. Perhaps you realize that your very words have built a wall between lovers rather than a bridge between friends. Is change possible? Absolutely!

If you've read my book *Becoming the Woman of His Dreams: Seven Qualities Every Man Longs For,* then you are familiar with the story of

Don and Jona. Jona experienced a dramatic change in the way she spoke to her husband; however, it was almost too late.

> Don was 27 years old when Jona first met him on a fall church beach retreat. Immediately, she knew he was exactly what she had always dreamed of in a husband. Don had a strong faith in God, a good job, a college degree, drive, and dreams for the future. He was physically fit, witty, adventurous, sexy, and just plain gorgeous. On top of that, he was constantly surrounded by women at the retreat who were vying for his attention.
>
> Jona could hardly believe her good fortune when Don asked her out upon their return home. Don and Jona dated only three months before he asked her to marry him, and before the spring beach retreat, on March 30, 1985, they were husband and wife.
>
> Their first year of marriage was a blissful blur of candlelight dinners, spontaneous lovemaking, and endless conversation. The icing on the one-year anniversary cake was the purchase of their first home. By their second anniversary, Don quit his job to start his own business. Life was clicking along at a steady pace toward acquiring the American Dream. By their third anniversary, Jona had their first child and joined the ranks of "stay-at-home mom." But after 24 months of Don's new business venture, the couple faced a second mortgage, a dwindling bank account, and looming personal loans. Jona was forced to go back to work, and seeds of discontentment, disrespect, and disenchantment began to take root.
>
> "I was so mad at Don for the mistakes I felt he had made," Jona explained. "Deep down, I wanted him to be God and to fulfill all my needs. He made a poor God. When my mother died, I sank into a clinical depression. I spent most of my time at home in bed. And even though I had two children by this time, I withdrew from being a mom as well

as being a wife. I then began to eat…and eat. I went from 140 pounds to 240 pounds.

"Don and I had the perfect engagement, a beautiful wedding, and a fantasy honeymoon. But when the obstacles came, I wasn't prepared. I thought, *This is not the way the story goes. What happened to the fairy tale?*

"Though Don changed jobs about every other year, he always provided for our needs. It just drove me crazy that he couldn't stay put.

"I remember one day Don said, 'Why are you eating and gaining all this weight?' I shot back, 'I'm doing this because I don't want you to touch me. Besides, I can lose the weight if I want to, but you'll always be a loser.' Little by little, word by word, angry look by angry look, rejection by rejection, I began the process of destroying my husband. Comments like 'You're so stupid,' 'Duh,' and 'Can't you do anything right?' were constantly spewing from my mouth. I was in pain and I wanted Don to be in pain too. One day I made a list of all of Don's faults. He found the list, but I didn't even care."

Jona always thought that because Don was a Christian, he would never leave her. However, there came a point where he couldn't take the emotional turmoil any longer. On May 6, 2001, Don left. Jona had single-handedly destroyed her marriage and her man. On January 31, 2003, the divorce was final.

"Shortly after Don left, I woke up to God's still, small voice," Jona explained. "He seemed to say, 'Is this what you wanted? Did you want a divorce? Do you want Don to marry another woman and have your children torn between spending time in two different households? Do you want to be alone?' 'Oh, God,' I cried, 'What have I done?'"

While Don and Jona were officially divorced, God was not

finished with either of them. God took Jona to a place of repentance and began to soften, remold, and remake her heart. That's what God does. He doesn't try to cover up our flaws; He starts from scratch and makes us new. While the divorce was final, God was only just beginning to work on Jona's heart.

"God took me to a place of repentance," she explained. "For the first time, through a support group, I saw clearly what I had done to destroy my marriage. I had always blamed our problems on Don changing jobs so often, but the real problem was my lack of respect for the God-appointed leader of my home. I was the real problem, and Don simply couldn't take it anymore. I had rejected him with my words, my appearance, and my withdrawal of physical touch."

Whether or not God could salvage the marriage, Jona made a commitment that she would allow God to salvage her.

Jona's heart longed to be reunited to Don, but her ultimate goal was to become the woman God wanted her to be. She immersed herself in Bible study and prayer, and she began to take an interest in her appearance. Interestingly, as the pounds began to drop, so did the scales that had covered her eyes.

"I began to understand what God's Word said about the relationship between a husband and wife. I was not Don's Holy Spirit. I was not the leader of my home. God had called me to respect Don as the leader, to honor him as a child of God, and to love him with my all. One day when Don came to pick up the boys, I shared with him what I had been learning.

"I told Don that I knew we were divorced, but I was making a commitment to submit to him. I didn't when we were married, but I did from that time forward.

" 'That's fine,' he told me. 'But you need to know I'm moving on with my life.'

"'You can move on,' I said, 'But I'm staying right here.'"

Jona continued to encourage Don and give him her BEST.

"BEST stands for bless, edify, share, and touch," she explained. "I began to touch him when he came by the house. I'd pat his back or give him a quick hug. When I knew he was coming, I'd put on a nice dress and fix my hair. I'd tell him I was proud of how he was handling the boys and share with him what God was teaching me. Some people told him I was trying to trick him and that he should ignore me, but it wasn't a trick. God had changed my heart, and I was committed, no matter what happened between us in the future, to never go back to being that woman I had been before.

"Sharon, I hate to tell you this," she said, "but for the first time I prayed for Don. I had never prayed for him before, but now I pray for him all the time."

Jona lost a hundred pounds and gained a beautiful, glowing countenance. It was amazing. More than the change in her physical appearance, the glow of Jesus Christ shone through her radiant face.

One day Don said, "Jona, you look soooo good."

"Don, I know I look better, but what I want you to see is my heart."

"I do see it, Jona," he said with tears in his eyes. "But, I'm moving on."

Jona knew that Don had met someone else, and while she never said a discouraging word about his new relationship, she continued to love Don and gave him her BEST. When her mind went to the other woman, God whispered, *You don't need to know the details. Leave that to Me. You just love him.*

Don was confused at times and a bit leery of the change. "Why do you think I'm wonderful all of a sudden?" he asked her.

"Because now I see you through God's eyes," she explained. "I see that you are a wonderful man."

Don fell in love with Jona all over again. No, it wasn't a trick—it was a miracle. God has given them a second chance. They were remarried on August 24, 2003. He is the God of second chances.

Dear friends, Jona has so graciously allowed me to tell you her story because she has decided that she will do anything to help even one woman not make the same mistakes she made. She cried and cried all through the recounting of the story and relived the pain for you. "God allowed me to go to a terrible place," Jona explained. "My prayer is that others will not have to go to that place before they wake up and realize what they are doing to their men."[7]

If you see a glimpse of yourself in Jona's story, please know that it is never too late to change! God brings life from death, and He can certainly give us the power to change the way we speak. Be encouraged, my friend. If you are willing to use your words to speak life into your marriage, He is more than able to supply the power to do so.

WORDS CAN MOTIVATE A MAN

Susan attended a class on how to appreciate her husband. Part of the assignment for the following week was to tell her husband something she admired about him. Her husband was quite handsome, but in all their years together she had never put her admiration into words. It was a big step for her. She didn't quite know how to start, even though she loved her husband. That evening while he was reading the paper, she sat down next to him on the sofa and began stroking his arm. After a bit, she stopped at the bicep and squeezed. He subconsciously flexed his muscle, and she said, "Oh, I never knew you were so muscular!" He put down the paper, looked at her, and asked, "What else?" He was so starved for admiration from his wife, he wanted to hear more.

How about your man? When was the last time you told him that you loved his smile or admired his talent? Can't remember? Well, today could be the day! That's your homework. Use your words to build up that man of yours. If you need a jump start, flip over to the end of the chapter for words your man longs to hear.

Sophia used her words to elevate and motivate her husband. One day he came home very discouraged and defeated. He had just lost his job and dreaded telling his wife the bad news. However, after explaining the situation, Sophia had an unexpected response. She was actually excited!

"Now," she said triumphantly as she clapped her hands in delight, "you can write your book!"

"Yes," replied the man, with sagging confidence. "And what shall we live on while I am writing it?"

To his amazement, she opened a drawer and pulled out a substantial amount of money.

"Where on earth did you get that?" he exclaimed.

"I have always known you were a man of genius," she told him. "I knew that someday you would write a masterpiece. So every week, out of the money you gave me to run the house, I saved a little bit. Here is enough to last us for one whole year."

From her trust, confidence, and encouraging words came one of the greatest novels of American literature. That was the year Nathaniel Hawthorne wrote *The Scarlet Letter*.[8]

What dreams does your man have hidden away in the recesses of his heart? How can you use your words to show him that you believe in him and help those dreams come true? It could be that all he needs is to hear the words, "I believe in you."

WORDS CAN CAPTIVATE A MAN

The book of Proverbs has much to say about wives and words:

> Like a gold ring in a pig's snout is a beautiful woman who shows no discretion (Proverbs 11:22).

> A quarrelsome wife is like the constant dripping of a leaky roof (Proverbs 19:13).

Better to live on a corner of the roof than share a house with a quarrelsome wife (Proverbs 21:9; worth repeating—Proverbs 25:24).

Better to live in a desert than with a quarrelsome and nagging wife (Proverbs 21:19).

A quarrelsome wife is like the dripping of a leaky roof in a rainstorm; restraining her is like restraining the wind or grasping oil with the hand (Proverbs 27:15-16).

Well, that's enough of that!

The book of Proverbs begins with a father warning his son against the ways of wicked women and ends with a mother teaching her son the blessings of finding a godly wife.

A wife of noble character who can find? She is worth far more than rubies. Her husband has full confidence in her and lacks nothing of value. She brings him good, not harm, all the days of her life…Her husband is respected at the city gate, where he takes his seat among the elders of the land… Her children arise and call her blessed; her husband also, and he praises her: "Many women do noble things, but you surpass them all" (Proverbs 31:10-12,23,28-29).

Can't you just see it now? Your husband is sitting at his desk, lost in thought about how blessed he is to have you as his wife. He holds your framed picture in his hand and moisture begins to pool in his eyes. He is captivated. *All the riches in the world are not to be compared with the jewel I have in this woman. What did I ever do to deserve her? God has given me such a gift. All our married life, she has done nothing but love me, bring out the best in me, and look out for my best interest. All the guys at the office are envious of our relationship. I see the way their eyes soften when she comes by just to tell me hello, grabs my hand when we're at office functions, or pecks me on the cheek for no apparent reason. I notice that her loving words to me are in stark contrast to some of the cutting remarks of other wives…and so do my friends. I look around at the accomplishments of my life, but having this woman as my wife is my greatest. Sure, there are many women out there in the world who are accomplishing great feats, but my wife…well, she surpasses them all.*

What a picture! That's the woman I want to be. Our words have the power to make it so.

POWER-PACKED WORDS

Twenty-Five Things a Husband Hopes He Never Hears

- I told you so.
- You're always in a bad mood.
- You just don't think.
- It's all your fault.
- What's wrong with you?
- All you ever do is complain.
- I can't do anything to please you.
- You made your bed; now lie in it.
- You should have thought about that before.
- You never listen to me.
- All you care about is yourself.
- I don't know why I put up with you.
- I can talk to you until I'm blue in the face, and it doesn't do any good.
- If you don't like it, you know where the door is.
- That was stupid.
- What's your problem?

- You think you're always right.

- You don't own me.

- You never help me around the house.

- Who do you think you are?

- You're impossible.

- What do you want now?

- You are such a big baby.

- It's all about you, isn't it?

- How many times do I have to tell you?

Twenty-Five Things
a Husband Longs to Hear

- I've been thinking about you all day.

- What can I do for you today?

- How can I pray for you today?

- The best part of my day is when you come home.

- You are one of God's most precious gifts to me.

- Thank you.

- I'm sorry.

- You are so wonderful.

- You look so handsome today.

- You make my day brighter.

- I don't feel complete without you.

- You are my best friend.

- I love spending time with you.

- Thank you for taking such good care of me.
- You are my knight in shining armor.
- I will always love you.
- I trust your decisions.
- I can always count on you.
- What would you like to do?
- I prize every moment we're together.
- I see God's fingerprints all over you.
- You are such an inspiration to so many people.
- You are such a wonderful father.
- You could give classes on how to be a great husband.
- I believe in you.

Come Sit by Me

THE POWER OF A WOMAN'S WORDS TO HER FRIENDS

Encouragement is oxygen to the soul.

GEORGE MATTHEW ADAMS

t was the worst phone call of Ann's life.

"Hello."

"Hey, Mom. This is Hugh."

"Hi, son. What are you doing calling me in the middle of the day? Is everything all right?"

"No, it's not. Can you come?"

During the summer after Hugh's freshman year in college, his mom watched helplessly as he sank into a deep depression. A dark cloud engulfed his emotions, and he couldn't see or feel his way out. Ann and her husband took what they felt were positive steps to help, but when they took Hugh back to school the following fall, everything in Ann cried out for her to wrap her arms around her son and keep him close.

Three months later the darkness became so bleak that Hugh knew he was in trouble and checked into a hospital. Trying to be a ray of sunshine to penetrate the darkness, Ann moved into a furnished apartment near his campus and spread her wings as a safe place for him to heal. They finished his semester together.

Why do I tell you this story in a section on friends? Because Ann said she could not have made it through that difficult year without an incredible gift of God…her friend Mary.

"God sent Mary to be His hands and feet, embracing arms, listening ear, and encouraging friend," Ann recalls. "It was Mary who made the hotel reservation for my husband and me as we quickly drove to the hospital. It was Mary who cried out to God on our behalf when I was too tired to kneel. It was Mary who reminded me that God was still on His throne and that He was good when I had times of doubt. It was Mary who understood because she had been there herself.

"When I didn't know what was going on in Hugh's mind, Mary could tell me what had transpired in her own when she struggled with depression," Ann continued. "When Hugh had no hope that life could ever be different than it was at that moment, it was Mary's words, a fellow sojourner and friend, who showed me otherwise. When I felt despair wash over me with its broad brush strokes of gray, Mary assured me that it would lift and the bright colors would eventually return."

Emily Dickinson once said, "Hope is the thing with feathers that perches in the soul—and sings the tune without words—and never stops at all." We can be the song of hope when a friend forgets the melody of her heart. Mary was that friend for Ann. That is the power of a woman's words to her friends.

FRIENDSHIP WAS GOD'S IDEA

We have already seen that when God said, "It is not good for the man to be alone," He created woman (Genesis 2:18). And while it isn't in the Bible, I think He must have thought, *It's not good for the woman to be alone*, so He created friends. All through the Bible we see how God brought women together for mutual support and companionship. Just as He brought Mary to Elizabeth and Ruth to Naomi, He still brings women together for mutual support, accountability, and friendship with bonds that last a lifetime.

Naomi in the Bible was a woman who lost everything important to her, except her closest friend. She was a young girl when she met and married Elimelech. His name meant "God is King," and she knew that he would always serve the living God of Israel. The young couple had two sons, whose names suggested they were somewhat of a disappointment: Mahlon meant "puny or weakling" and Kilion meant "pining."

When the boys were still young lads, a famine struck the area surrounding Bethlehem, and the city whose name meant "House of Bread" had no bread to feed its own. So Elimelech packed up his family of four and headed to Moab in hopes of better days.

We are not sure of the details that followed, but we do know that both boys married Moabite women. Over the next ten years Elimelech, Mahlon, and Kilion died, leaving Naomi alone with her two Moabite daughters-in-law. Downcast, defeated, and discouraged, Naomi decided to return to her homeland and her people. The famine had passed, and even though there was no hope of grandchildren to carry on her family name, or a husband or son to care for her in her twilight years, at least she would be among familiar faces.

"Girls," Naomi said one day, "I have heard news from my homeland. God has remembered Bethlehem and the famine has passed. There is no reason for me to stay in Moab, and I have decided to return to the land of my people. I want you both to go back to your mother's house and find other nice young men to marry. I pray God will be as kind to you as you have been to me."

Naomi kissed each of the girls as they wept loudly. "We will go back with you to your people," they cried.

"No, my daughters," Naomi said. "Go back home. There's no reason for you to come with me. I know it is the custom for you to marry another son in a family if your husband dies, but I'm not going to have any more sons. Even if I did, I wouldn't want you to wait around until they were old enough to marry. Now, go back to your mother's house. That is the best solution. The Lord's hand has gone out against me. My dreams are buried with Elimelech, Mahlon, and Kilion."

The two women loved their mother-in-law dearly and wept bitterly. After what seemed like hours, one of the girls, Orpah, kissed her mother-in-law goodbye and turned to walk away. The other girl, Ruth, clung to Naomi's robe and begged to go with her.

"Don't urge me to leave you or to turn back from you. Where you

go I will go, and where you stay I will stay. Your people will be my people and your God my God. Where you die I will die, and there I will
be buried. May the LORD deal with me, be it ever so severely, if even
death separates you and me" (Ruth 1:16-17).

Naomi and Ruth both knew that most Israelites despised Moabites.
The Israelites had never forgiven the Moabites for hiring Balaam to
place a curse on them after they left Egypt for the Promised Land many
years before (Numbers 22:1-6). Yet, regardless of the opposition Ruth
knew she would face, she still desired to go and take care of her friend.

So Naomi relented and allowed Ruth to return with her. After the
arduous journey, the dusty and exhausted women arrived at their des-
tination. The twosome caused quite a stir, and the townspeople began
to whisper among themselves, "Could this be Naomi? It looks like her,
and yet it doesn't."

She was so depressed that her very countenance disguised the
woman she had been before. Naomi heard the whispers as she walked
by and stopped in her tracks. "Don't call me Naomi [which means
pleasant]," she told them. "Call me Mara [which means bitter], because
the Almighty has made my life very bitter. I went away full, but the
LORD has brought me back empty. Why call me Naomi? The LORD has
afflicted me; the Almighty has brought misfortune upon me" (Ruth
1:20-21).

I imagine Ruth felt a pang in her heart at the words "brought me
back empty." Part of her must have thought, *What about me? Don't I
count for something?* But the other part of her knew Naomi was speaking out of her loss and pain. Naomi was blinded by bitterness and didn't
recognize hope walking right beside her in the form of a Moabite girl.

All through the book of Ruth, we see how God used this daughter-in-law to encourage her forlorn friend. She went out into the field
to glean barley to feed her, she lent a listening ear to console her, and
she offered words to soothe her. God even used Ruth to jog Naomi's
memory and remind her that she was not alone in the world. She had
a kinsman-redeemer by the name of Boaz, a distant relative who was
more than willing—yes, even eager—to care for her. Boaz married the
widow Ruth, and together they placed hope in Naomi's arms...a baby

boy by the name of Obed. Maybe you're not familiar with the name Obed, but I bet you've heard of his grandson—the most powerful king in Israel's history, King David.

I suspect that Naomi asked her friends to stop calling her Mara after Ruth married Boaz and gave her a grandson. I imagine she reclaimed her title of "pleasant." Her friends proclaimed, "Praise be to the LORD, who this day has not left you without a guardian-redeemer. May he become famous throughout Israel! He will renew your life and sustain you in your old age. For your daughter-in-law, who loves you and who is better to you than seven sons, has given him birth" (Ruth 4:14-15).

When Naomi returned to town, her old acquaintances were shocked at her downcast appearance. She had gone away married and wealthy, but she returned home widowed and poor. However, we see no signs that they offered to alleviate her pain or assist her situation. They wagged their tongues in gossip but didn't lift a hand to lighten her load.

On the contrary, Ruth gives us a wonderful example of how to care for a broken-spirited friend. She didn't reprimand Naomi by telling her to "snap out of it," scold her by reminding her of all she had to be thankful for, or shame her by telling her to stop feeling sorry for herself. She didn't berate her with words such as, "You're not the only one suffering around here, you know. I lost my husband too!"

No, Ruth loved Naomi unconditionally, cared for her unceasingly, and supported her unselfishly. Ruth is a wonderful example of Paul's words to the Galatians: "Rejoice with those who rejoice, and weep with those who weep" (Romans 12.15 NASB). Interestingly, *Ruth* means "woman friend."

Have you ever noticed that hurting people hurt people? Many times a friend in pain may toss words about like darts, and the whole world becomes the target. A wise woman extends grace to a hurting friend, knowing that her words are being filtered through a sieve of pain. I imagine Ruth endured more than being ignored…perhaps she served as the target for pointed words as well. Yet she was persistent and consistent in her love for Naomi.

Galatians 6:2 says, "Carry each other's burdens." The word *burdens* is more appropriately translated "overburdens."[1] It is more than simply having too many errands to run, a dirty house that needs cleaning, or a never-ending pile of laundry. An overburden is when the burdens of life grow too heavy for someone to carry alone, such as the loss of a spouse, the death of a family member, the rebellion of a teen, the termination of a job, the bad report from a biopsy, or chronic illness.

Ruth gives us an example of how to bear someone's burden. She took care of Naomi's emotional needs by simply staying with her, her physical needs by providing food for her, and her spiritual needs by reminding her of the providence of God. It all began with her words— a declaration of determination and love: "Don't urge me to leave you or turn back from you. Where you go I will go, and where you stay I will stay. Your people will be my people and your God my God. Where you die I will die, and there I will be buried" (Ruth 1:16-17). In other words, "Naomi, I'm not leaving you, so just forget about it. You are my friend, and I'm in this relationship for the long haul. You can't get rid of me by simply moving out of town. I'm coming with you!"

Naomi's circumstances were dire, but any friendship will experience periods when someone hits a dry spell and is not able to give much to the relationship. The test of a true friend is whether or not we can love enough to wait it out. Walter Winchell once said, "A friend is one who walks in when others walk out."

What if a hurting friend shuts you out as Naomi tried to shut her two daughters-in-law out of her life? We can choose, like Orpah, to turn and walk away. Or we can choose, like Ruth, to stick close by.

Ruth was in pain, and yet she was able to focus on her dear friend. She lived up to her name. She gives us a vivid example of how to hold an emotional umbrella over a friend through the storms of life.

God still brings women together for mutual support, accountability, and friendship with bonds that last a lifetime.

WORDS THAT BREATHE
LIFE INTO THE WEARY

When I was in my teens, I went scuba diving with some friends. I had no training and probably shouldn't have been in deep water, but I was a teenager and threw caution to the wind. The guy who took me below the surface of the deep—another teenager, I might add—strapped an oxygen tank on his back, a mask on his face, and flippers on his feet. I only had a mask and flippers.

"Where's my oxygen?" I asked.

"I've got it," he answered as he patted the tank on his back.

So into the ocean we jumped. He put his arm around my waist as though I were a sack of potatoes and down we went. John drew oxygen from the tank and then passed the breathing apparatus to me. We took turns breathing in the oxygen in what he called "buddy breathing." It then occurred to me that I was totally dependent on this boy to keep me alive!

This was not a very smart idea, but it did leave me with a great life lesson…"Buddy Breathing." Throughout my life, the words of my friends have been like oxygen when I felt as though I was drowning. Even today, I have a mental scrapbook of the life-giving words passed along to me when I felt I was suffocating.

In high school, I traveled to Europe with a group of students to study abroad. My family was falling apart, and it felt like a good time to take a break from all the tension. The difficult part was leaving my groups of strong Christian friends who constantly breathed life into me and kept me afloat. However, God was trying to teach me how to swim on my own.

Before I left, my group of Christian girlfriends gave me a gift. They had taken a large medicine bottle and filled it with a homemade remedy. A handwritten label was taped to the outside with the following instructions:

For: Miss Sharon Edwards PBP 71240

Take as needed for uplifting of the spirit.

May be followed by faith and prayer for faster relief.

Vitamin PTLa

Filled by SIC

Inside the medicine bottle were 100 Bible verses written on small strips of paper and rolled up like tiny scrolls. These verses were my medicine. The "pharmacists" were my Sisters in Christ, and the vitamins were Praise the Lord anyway brand. That gift of the heart was given to me more than 40 years ago, and I've carried them with me through high school, college, marriage, and many, many moves. I have kept that bottle of love with me at each crossroad and bend in the road. That's the power of a woman's words to her friends. We never know how a small act of kindness will touch someone's heart for many years to come.

Kim discovered this simple fact when she was sinking to the bottom of her emotional sea. "I was probably at the lowest place emotionally and spiritually I had been since asking Jesus into my heart," Kim explained. "I call it my 'tomb time,' a time of loneliness, darkness, and death."

God seemed distant and aloof to Kim, and life was just not turning out like she had hoped. She doubted her abilities, her faith, and her relationships.

"During this period, I ran into an old friend I hadn't seen for a while," Kim continued. "I admired her so much. Sue was a few years older than me, and just the kind of woman I always wanted to be. She noticed my sad countenance and asked what was going on in my life. I shared the details of my pain, and she wrapped me in her arms and in prayer."

A few days later, Kim received a letter from Sue. She quoted Isaiah 42:3: "A bruised reed He will not break and a dimly burning wick He will not extinguish" (NASB). At the bottom of the letter Sue wrote four simple, powerful words: "I believe in you."

"I wept when I read those words," Kim remembered. "Amazingly, tears still swell when I think of her words today. I couldn't believe in myself, but this woman, whom I loved and admired, believed in me. Those words set me on a course of hope that somehow life would get better…and it did. God is faithful and I am so grateful He sent Sue to give me hope. Even today, when I feel bruised or that my light is a bit dim, I sense God's hands surrounding me to keep me from breaking or my little light from blowing out, and I remember that my dear friend believes in me. God's hands and Sue's heart—that's all I need to press on until the sun shines again. I remember the power of those words, and I have spoken and written them to others, hoping they too will be encouraged to press on."

As Kim told me her story, tears brimmed in her eyes. The incident occurred 27 years ago.

I've noticed through the years that a true friend is one who knows what I need without me even asking. She is someone who will offer to pitch in and help when she sees me growing weary. A true friend never sees the mess in my house, but the love in my eyes. She listens without judging, but sets me straight when she sees me straying off course. She never ridicules my children or my husband, and encourages me to love them better. She doesn't simply say, "I'll pray for you," but rather, "Let's stop and pray right now." A true friend says, "I believe in you, and I'll be the first to blow the horn at your celebration party!"

King Solomon painted a beautiful portrait of the power of a woman's words to her friends in Ecclesiastes 4:9-10,12:

> Two are better than one, because they have a good return for their labor: If either of them falls down, one can help the other up. But pity anyone who falls and has no one to help them up!…A cord of three strands is not quickly broken.

We can embrace a friend with words that warm a chilled soul, words that fill an empty heart, and words that lift her up when she is lying facedown in defeat. I'm so glad that friendship was God's idea.

WORDS THAT BRACE UP THE WEAK

It was just a bit of burlap peeking out from underneath the soil, but to our golden retriever, Ginger, it was a challenge that needed to be conquered.

Shortly after we had planted a maple tree in our backyard, we went on vacation. It was the first time we had left Ginger home alone, and a neighbor fed and watched out for her while we were away. On the second day of our trip, I called Cathy to see how Ginger was doing.

"Well, Ginger's fine," Cathy reported. "But you know that tree you planted last week? She dug it up!"

"She did what!" I exclaimed.

"She dug it up. The tree's lying in the yard."

When we got home, we walked over to the toppled tree. Ginger tucked her tail and slunk into the garage.

When we planted the tree, we left a small piece of the burlap around the root ball exposed. Ginger spied that remnant peeking out of the ground and wanted it…bad. Several times we had caught her pawing at the burlap and reprimanded her with a stern "no!" She ducked her head, crept away, and waited for a more opportune time.

I imagine that the moment she saw us load suitcases in the car and pull out of the driveway, she tiptoed over to the forbidden tree and began to dig. (Can dogs tiptoe? I think they can.) She must have dug and dug for hours with all her puppy might—flinging dirt in every direction. *I've got to get to the bottom of this,* she might have thought. *This must be exposed!*

Finally, she accomplished her mission, and the burlap was totally uncovered! Exposed! Of course, she gave no thought to the tree she toppled in the meantime. It was never about the tree.

As I stared at the poor little maple lying helplessly in the hot summer sun, I thought about how many friends, and myself for that matter, have been in the same state—toppled and left to wither in the heat of glaring eyes. Perhaps someone has a little flaw that peeks through the surface of his or her character. Then someone else comes along and decides that the flaw is a nuisance and must be exposed at all cost. That someone starts digging and digging—flinging dirt in every direction with no thought as to what all the digging is doing to the person's heart. Before you know it, the rough burlap—the unsightly character flaw— is unearthed and exposed for all to see. And the victim of that digging lies toppled in the process. Lifeless, wounded, exposed—and for what purpose? To satisfy someone's dogged determination to uncover a rough edge?

There are times in any friendship when confrontation is necessary, but we must always make sure that the confrontation is wrapped in prayer and tied with the ribbon of love. If we take any joy whatsoever in the process, then we must stop and check our motives and attitude.

Ann Hibbard, in her book *Treasured Friends,* describes the difference between a friend who tends to dig us up and one who tries to hold us up:

> A true friend is someone we look to for support. She is always on our team, cheering us on to victory. When we have a problem, she does not try to solve it for us. Instead, she listens and expresses her solidarity. When our perspective has become distorted by self-pity, she encourages us, not with pat answers but by gently pointing us toward the truth.

There is never a hint of criticism from a true friend. That doesn't mean she doesn't sometimes say hard things. She is the one who asks the tough questions. But we know that her intentions for us are only good. Anyone can say what we want to hear. A true friend tells us what we need to hear. Yet, every word is prompted by love.[2]

Steve and I gently removed what was left of the burlap sack around the root system, carefully sat the maple back up into her prepared soil, and lovingly patted the dirt back around her parched roots. Then, because of her weakened state, we braced her up with ropes tied to three stakes in the ground. I watered the weary maple daily, not knowing if she would recover from the trauma. In the end, the tree not only survived, she thrived.

Oh, that we would do the same for our toppled friends. When we see a friend who has been wounded by words, we can slowly stand her back up, lovingly reestablish her roots in the good soil of God's Word, gently brace her up with kindness, and water her daily with prayer. Who knows? You may even help her not only survive, but thrive.

Thankfully, Ginger left the tree alone after that episode. After all, she never cared about the tree in the first place.

WORDS THAT STAND IN THE GAP

One night I was in the restroom touching up my makeup before speaking to several hundred women. I was having one of those moments when I looked in the mirror and my thoughts began to swirl in my mind. *What am I doing here? What do I possibly have to say to these women that could make any difference in their lives? I am not capable of walking to that podium tonight.*

While I was mulling over the lies, the fiery darts that Satan was shooting into my mind, my cell phone rang.

"Hello."

"Hi, Sharon. This is Mary. Where are you?"

"Actually, I'm standing in the restroom at a speaking engagement getting ready to walk out on the stage. I forgot to turn off my cell phone!"

"I want you to know," Mary continued, "that God interrupted me while I was cooking dinner and told me to pray for you. Not only that, He told me to call you now."

I was imagining Mary standing in her kitchen with spaghetti sauce simmering on the stove and stopping midstir. There might have been a little conversation with God that went something like this: *Call Sharon and pray for her,* God might have said.

Could You just wait a minute, God? The sauce is almost done.

Call Sharon and pray for her.

Okay, okay, I'll do it now.

There was great power in Mary's instant obedience. If she had waited, I would not have known she was praying. Not only did God prompt her to pray at that moment, He wanted her to tell me she was doing so. Why? God knew there was power in her prayer, and He wanted me to know that I was not going into battle alone. He had prompted Mary to stand in the gap for me—to struggle in prayer for me and strive together with me. In that one moment, Mary and I locked our shields of faith through words, and marched into battle together.

The prophet Ezekiel recorded these words from God in Ezekiel 22:30: "I looked for someone among them who would build up the wall and stand before me in the gap on behalf of the land so I would not have to destroy it, but I found no one." These words were referring to God looking for someone to pray for, or stand in the gap for sinful Jerusalem, but I believe we can apply them to our lives as well. Did you notice that God said, "I looked for *someone*"? It could be that you are that *someone*, or I am that *someone*, who could use our words to stand in the gap for a friend.

Paul understood the power of our words as we stand in the gap for our friends. He implored his friends to pray for him: "I urge you, brothers and sisters, by our Lord Jesus Christ and by the love of the Spirit, to join me in my struggle by praying to God for me" (Romans 15:30). "Pray also for me, that whenever I speak, words may be given me so that I will fearlessly make known the mystery of the gospel, for which I am an ambassador in chains. Pray that I may declare it fearlessly, as I should" (Ephesians 6:19-20).

The New Testament was originally written in Greek, and sometimes looking at the original definitions of the words can give us great insight. The Greek word Paul uses for *struggle* in Romans 15:30 is *sunagonizomai,* which means "to struggle in company of; i.e., to be a partner (assistant), strive together with."[3] The root word means "to endeavor to accomplish something: fight, labor fervently, strive." For example, to compete for a prize or to contend with an adversary.[4]

Prayer for another person is not simply a nice platitude or a pat on the back. When we tell someone we will pray for them, we are agreeing to put on the armor and head to the front lines of battle on their behalf.

Many ancient shields had brackets attached to the sides. These brackets were a type of latch that soldiers used to lock their shields together during battle. When locked together, the soldiers moved as one, forming a barricade against the enemy. Alone, the shield was a small defense. Hooked together, they were a human wall. Do you see the significance? When we lock arms in prayer with our friends, we are locking our shields together and forming a powerfully strong wall of defense. That's what Mary did for me that night through the phone lines. That's what we can do for our friends.

Stop right now and ask God who He is calling you to pray for today. Then send her a text or give her a call and let her know.

WORDS THAT SHARPEN
AND CHALLENGE

Dale Carnegie, author of *How to Win Friends and Influence People,* said, "You can make more friends in two months by becoming interested in other people than you can in two years by trying to get people interested in you."[3] Everyone has an inborn need to feel significant. When we listen to a friend and engage in conversation with questions that show we're interested in their lives, then that person feels that they matter in this world. The Bible teaches, "Let us consider how we may spur one another on toward love and good deeds" (Hebrews 10:24).

In my silverware drawer at home, I have about 15 knives of various shapes and sizes. However, I only use about four of them, and the others simply are taking up space. The problem is, the other knives are dull, and I've never taken the time to sharpen them. I should just toss them in the trash. They're certainly not doing anybody any good.

The same can be true in our own lives. The Bible says, "As iron sharpens iron, so one person sharpens another" (Proverbs 27:17). When we don't have friends that challenge us and encourage us to grow, we become dull. Ultimately, we become "not the sharpest knife in the drawer," and others are chosen for tasks that we would love to do. But we have to be careful. Sharpening must always be done in love.

Bonnie is one of my friends who keeps me sharp. Her sometimes brutal honesty is couched in such love for me that I can take the sharpening even if it hurts. It is a tough love that I have grown to appreciate and admire. Sometimes her honesty makes me burst out laughing.

Bonnie and I don't live in the same state, and we take every opportunity to squeeze in a visit. One weekend we both attended the same meeting and shared a hotel room together. After an exhausting day of seminars, Bonnie and I were snuggled in our adjacent beds chatting. I confided in her about an internal struggle I was having with a particular person.

"That's just plain old sin," Bonnie said.

"What?" I asked.

"Sharon, that's sin. You need to pray about that," she flatly replied.

I have to tell you, I laughed till I cried. Who else but Bonnie would call a spade a spade and label my whining for exactly what it was? I love her to pieces. She's not afraid to pull out the sharpening stone when she notices I'm getting a bit dull.

But everyone can't be a Bonnie in our lives, and we certainly can't be a Bonnie to everyone in our lives. That's a surefire way to lose friends and alienate people.

Bonnie has earned the right to sharpen me because she loves me well. Likewise, we can't go around expecting to use our words to sharpen others around us without loving them first. We have to earn the right.

One day I conducted an experiment. Actually, it was not intentional, but very effective. I sent out my weekly blog without proofing it. Bad idea. When the blog posted on my website, it had several typos. *Oh, well,* I thought, *Grace, grace, grace.*

But the interesting part of the pseudo experiment was the e-mail responses I received. One woman wrote back, "Check your spelling! Run a grammar check!" Another woman wrote back, "Today's blog meant so much to me. Thank you for ministering to me through your words." Then another wrote, "Sharon, I just hate to see typos in your wonderful blogs. I know you are busy. Here's an idea. Why don't you send your blogs to me and I will proof them for you?"

As I looked at those e-mails, I saw the power of a woman's words to her friends encapsulated in those three responses.

One woman simply pointed out my faults.

One woman overlooked my faults and encouraged me in the ways I had blessed her.

One woman acknowledged my faults, encouraged me in the ways I had blessed her, and then went one step further. She offered to help.

We can be one of those three types of friends. We can be the type who simply points out faults, the type who overlooks the faults and focuses on the positives, or the type who praises someone's strengths and offers to help their weakness with the sharpening stone of love.

We all make mistakes, just different ones. The prophet Isaiah wrote, "We all, like sheep, have gone astray" (Isaiah 53:6). The philosopher

Goethe remarked, "One has only to grow older to become more tolerant. I see no fault that I might not have committed myself."

If we feel that we must use our words to exhort or correct a friend, we should be keenly aware that there are most likely areas in our own lives that need correcting as well. Jesus said,

> Why do you look at the speck of sawdust in your brother's eye and pay no attention to the plank in your own eye? How can you say to your brother, "Let me take the speck out of your eye," when all the time there is a plank in your own eye? You hypocrite, first take the plank out of your own eye, and then you will see clearly to remove the speck from your brother's eye (Matthew 7:3-5).

I am not suggesting that we withhold the sharpening tool when it is needed, but just make sure it is well oiled with love and a gentle spirit before the rub begins.

As women, we love to soak in warm bubble baths, lather in fragrant soaps, and soften with aromatic oils. But all too often, when it comes to removing dirt from a friend, we pull out the hard-bristled scrub brush of harsh words and scrub, scrub, scrub. The end result is often not the removal of dirt, but an abraded and chafed soul crying out for the soothing balm of a caring friend. Powerful words are not caustic words. They are gentle, tender words wrapped in an attitude of love. Paul wrote to the Colossians, "As God's chosen people, holy and dearly loved, clothe yourselves with compassion, kindness, humility, gentleness and patience" (Colossians 3:12). Clothe yourself in love. Wrap your words in love.

WORDS THAT INSPIRE
TO KEEP PRESSING ON

My son was fast, and he ran with a fast crowd. As a matter of fact, his entire track team was fast! In the ninth grade, Steven participated in the conference track meet, running the 1600 meters. (That's four times around the big circle.) I was so proud of him as he ran like a gazelle around the first lap, about six feet behind the first-place contestant. But at the beginning of the second lap, we saw an unidentified flying object soar over Steven's head.

"What was that?" my husband asked.

"I think it was his shoe!" I replied with amusement.

All the fans were laughing and pointing as they noticed Steven's left running shoe fly heavenward and land on the grassy field. But amazingly, Steven kept running and never missed a step. With one shoe off and one shoe on, he continued around the track. The atmosphere of the race lit with excitement, and the focus seemed to change. It became less about who would win and more about if shoeless Steven would make it to the finish line. All curious eyes were now on one lean runner. Would he stop? Would he slow down? Would his sock stay on?

His teammates began to run around the track, cheering him on. "Come on, Steven! Don't give up! Don't slow down! Keep going!"

Surprisingly, at the urging of his teammates, Steven sped up. By the third lap, he had passed the first-place runner by several paces. But then, predictably, his sock started to work its way down the ankle and the toe was flopping like a loose sole of a worn old shoe. Undaunted, Steven ran on, sock flopping.

When Steven crossed the finish line in first place, the crowd erupted in applause and laughter. He had broken his personal best running time!

"Son, maybe you should have kicked off both shoes," my husband chuckled. "No tellin' how fast you could have run. You made your best time ever. What made the difference?"

"I knew everybody was watching me," Steven answered. "It wasn't just a race anymore; they were watching to see what I'd do. It made me go faster. It made me want to do better."

All through our lives, we will notice friends, or "fellow runners," who have lost more than a shoe—they have lost their hopes, their dreams, and their will to finish the race. What will we do? What can we do? We can cheer them on by offering a timely word of encouragement and running alongside them shouting, "Come on, friend! Don't give up! Don't slow down! Keep going!"

Who knows, that friend may do more than simply finish the race. She may even take first place! Let's look for a friend who has lost her shoe. Well, maybe not a shoe, but her hope. Then run alongside her, encouraging her not to give up, but finish the race.

WORDS THAT PUT A SMILE
ON SOMEONE'S FACE

Even when I'm tucked away on my patio behind my house, I can tell when a neighbor is going for a walk or a jogger is running down the street. It starts with Mitzi, the white cockapoo one block away. Yip. Yip. Yip. Then it moves two houses down with Duchess, the black Labrador. Bow. Wow. Wow. The wave continues to move closer with Pal, the standard poodle. Arf. Arf. Arf. And on to Sprout, the collie. Woof. Woof. Woof.

Finally, the pedestrian turns onto my side street. Suddenly, the doggie hallelujah chorus breaks out with Alice, the white Lab, and Maple, the Heinz 57 across the street, and Duchess, the German shepherd next door. I usually don't see the passerby, but I can surely hear the barking from the dogs as he or she walks the route.

When I take my routine three-mile walk through the neighborhood, I am also greeted by the wave of barking dogs indignant that I should dare pass by their turf. I try not to let it hurt my feelings. However, the chain reaction of barking, growling, and gnashing of teeth always unnerves me.

The truth is, I wish the pups would wag their tails as I walk by as if to say, "Oh, there's that sweet Mrs. Jaynes. My, how I like her. I wish she were my master and we could take walks together. Mrs. Jaynes! Mrs. Jaynes! Won't you please come over and pat my head?" I wish they would run up to the fence, jump up sweetly, and rest their paws, beckoning me to stop for a visit. But for the 20 years I walked the same route, that never happened. It was always growl, yap, and bark. You'd think I would have gotten used to the barking, but I never did.

I hate to admit it, but it's been the same way in life from time to time. As I've walked down the path of years, especially down that road less traveled, I have heard some unfriendly barking, some disapproving yapping, and a few discoursing growls. I bet you have too. Sometimes it's a complaint because I'm not living up to someone's expectations. Sometimes it's because I'm not following someone else's plan for my life. And sometimes it's because I'm coloring outside people-imposed lines.

But let's just stop and call it what it is. Barking. Honestly, some humans just need to wear bark collars.

Thankfully, among the barking from the dogs in my neighborhood are a few friendly greetings. "Good morning, Sharon," a friend calls out from watering her garden. "Have a good day," a neighbor calls as she passes by on her way to work. "Hi, Mrs. Jaynes," a boy shouts as he speeds by on his bike. These are the words I treasure along the way.

As friends, we have the opportunity to cheer someone on during their busy day or simply bark, yap, and growl. A good friend will use her words to welcome others, not make them want to leave.

I have often heard that there are two types of people: those who brighten a room when they enter and those who brighten a room when they leave. The barking, whiny ones take the dark cloud with them when they leave. The positive, cheery ones reflect God's light when they arrive. That's the woman I want to be.

POWER-PACKED WORDS

Words a Friend
Would Love to Hear

Jesus taught, "Treat others as you want them to treat you" (Luke 6:31 TLB). Make a list of words that *you* would like to hear, and then use those same words to speak life into someone else. If there are words you would like to hear, chances are there are others out there who would like to hear them too.

Below are some of my favorites:

- You bring out the best in me.

- You are an inspiration to me.

- I love to hear how God is working in your life.
- How can I pray for you today?
- I can help you with that.
- I'd like your opinion.
- What do you think?
- You teach me so much about friendship.
- You inspire me to be a better person.
- You are a great wife, mother, friend, etc.
- Can I bring dinner to you tonight?
- I believe in you.
- You can accomplish anything God has called you to do.
- I am so glad we are friends.
- Yep, you made a mistake. Now, let's put it behind us and move on.
- You won't see me throwing the first stone.
- We all make mistakes.
- Thank you for…
- I am hurting with you.
- I don't understand either.
- Will you help me _____? You are so good at it.
- What can I do to help you reach your goal?
- You are such a great friend.
- I have learned so much from you.
- I want to be like you when I grow up.

Cheering from the Sidelines

THE POWER OF A WOMAN'S WORDS TO HER ADULT CHILDREN

Think all you speak, but speak not all you think.

PATRICK DELANEY

You might notice that I didn't put this chapter right after the one about speaking to children. That was intentional. The words we speak to our adult children should be more analogous to the words we speak to our friends than the way we spoke to them as kids, so I wanted you to have the "friends" chapter first. Much of that applies with adult children.

Various psychologists and authors have written about the stages of parenthood. Bob Hostetler calls these stages the Commander Phase (ages 1-5), the Coaching Phase (ages 6-12), the Counselor Phase (ages 13-18), and the Consultant Phase (ages 19 and beyond).[1] Another resource refers to them as the Loving Discipline Stage, the Training Stage, the Coaching Stage, and the Friendship Stage.[2] Whichever labels you choose, all agree that adult children fit into a category all their own, and if that rudder on the ship that James speaks of in 3:4 doesn't change direction, we're headed for rough waters.

Hostetler said this about the final stage:

No words adequately describe the jumble of emotions a parent experiences driving away from a child's freshman college dorm. It's frightening on so many levels. But it's less frightening if the parent has successfully navigated the first three phases. The task of parenting isn't done at this stage; it is no longer one of proactive involvement but of patient availability. Like Solomon, who told his son, "Be wise, my son, and bring joy to my heart" (Proverbs 27:11), the parent in this phase must hope, pray and wait.

Each phase has its own challenges, but phase four can be the most difficult because it requires letting go. For nearly two decades, the parent has been the child's commander, coach or counselor, but trying to prolong any of those roles will invite resistance and perhaps even resentment. As I did in the other phases, I found a phrase that has helped my interactions with my children: "Let me know if I can help." It allowed me to affirm my availability while respecting my children's independence.[3]

The bottom line is that when children morph into young adults, a parent's words need to morph right along with them. Failure to see and treat the grown child as an adult friend will ruin a relationship, sometimes beyond repair.

IT'S COMPLICATED

I've always thought responding to someone's question with, "It's complicated," was a total cop-out. It's like saying, "I just don't want to talk about it" or "You could never understand." But a woman's words to her adult children *are* complicated. There are so many variables to consider when talking to these creatures...of which I am one. Let's look at just a few.

First: I've already said that we should speak to adult children more like we would to a friend rather than a child. Parents often fantasize about being best friends with their adult children. And while the relationship may have many facets of a great friendship, there are differences. We get to choose our friends. We don't get to choose our children. And once you've got them, you can't send them back for a more compatible model. A parent invests time, emotions, money, and energy in a child year after year. Parents are nowhere near as invested in a friendship as they are with their children. If a friend disappoints or hurts us, we can opt out of the relationship. Not so with children! Parenthood is permanent. As Elizabeth Stone has put it, "Making the decision to have a child—it is momentous. It is to decide forever to have your heart go walking around outside your body." But at some point, we have to allow that heart to beat on its own.

Second: Most of the time our friends are like us. We have similar interests, opinions, worldviews, and hobbies. Not so with adult children. An adult child may be drastically different from his or her parents with opposite political, social, and moral beliefs. Their hobbies, interests, and goals may have no commonalities. An adult child may make lifestyle choices that run opposed to what they were taught under the parents' roof. At some point, the parents may wonder where in the world this person came from, and who kidnapped that compliant ten-year-old and replaced him with this bigger, older, vastly different version. The relational transformation from child to adult is like a tadpole morphing into a frog, where the last phase is sometimes unrecognizable from the first.

Another factor in deciphering the "adult child speak" code is personality differences. A mom can say the same thing to two different adult children and get two different responses. One adult child interprets a mom saying, "Do you want me to help you with your laundry?" as a welcome offer to relieve pressure of running a home. Another adult child hears that same statement and interprets it as, "You're not capable of keeping up with the housework. I don't like how you're so messy. You need me to step in and take over." I know. It's complicated. Another mom told me about how her four daughters responded to the simple words, "Drive safe," when they left her house. Three of the girls interpreted her farewell as a loving "goodbye." The fourth interpreted it as "You don't think I'm a good driver." The key is to understand the adult child's tendencies and craft our words carefully. And even then, what works in one situation may not work in another.

Another piece of the puzzle is that boys and girls—rather, men and women—perceive words differently. Stereotypically, men tend to take words at face value while women tend to wonder what you really mean. Birth order can also come into play. A straightforward firstborn may tend to receive words differently from the sensitive middle child. Is your head spinning yet?

And finally, we can't ignore the fact that words are filtered through the sieve of past hurts and hurdles. Did a child experience abandonment or bullying as a child? Did the adolescent experience drug addiction or sexual abuse? Did the young adult experience bankruptcy, rejection, or loss? Even as an adult myself, I have to always ask myself if I am interpreting others' words through the filter of past pain. Past experiences affect present perception.

Sometimes parents become so frustrated and confused about how to use their words with grown children, they just give up and float along, letting the words take them where they will. I have a better idea. While we aren't to use our words to necessarily steer the adult child, we can use our words to steer the relationship between us. Then if they feel safe and secure enough to ask for direction, we can make suggestions and pull out the map of wisdom and past experience.

By now I'm sure you can agree: *It's complicated.* With that said, this chapter is going to be a little different from the others. I'll give some general guidelines and suggestions that I've gleaned from interviewing adult children. I've interviewed mostly millennials and Gen Xers because those are the wonderful creatures that many holding this book will be talking to. The other group reading this book are the millennials and Gen Xers themselves—if that's the case, you might want your mom to read this chapter as well. So let's look at what to say, when to say it, and when to say nothing at all.

*Past experiences affect
present perception.*

ROBBING THE ADULT CHILD OF
THE JOY OF ACCOMPLISHMENT

As children we learn many cute little sayings: "Early to bed, early to rise, makes a man healthy, wealthy, and wise." "Don't put all your eggs in one basket." "Don't burn your bridges." I remember one childhood adage I recited as the neighborhood boys mercilessly teased me: "Sticks and stones may break my bones, but words will never hurt me." That's simply a big, fat lie. The pain of hurtful words lingers long after the pain of a broken bone is forgotten. Whether it's mean girls taunting a schoolmate in the lunchroom or a mom demeaning an adult child, the echoes can linger for a lifetime.

Bob told me about how his mother's hurtful words had clung to his heart for many years. When he was in his twenties, he worked in a family business with his father. He was very diligent and won recognition as the "Young Businessman of the Year." He, his young bride, and his parents traveled to Washington, DC, where he would accept his award. He sat eagerly at the dinner table, anticipating hearing his name announced from the podium. Then his mother leaned over and said, "You need to thank your father for this. You didn't really earn this award, you know. Your father earned it for you."

Bob's mom poked the pin of criticism into the balloon of his accomplishment, and his self-worth lay shriveled on the ballroom floor. He walked to the podium when his name was called, but the smile on his face masked the ache in his heart. That comment was the final nail in their relational coffin. Moms should never pat their own backs for their adult children's accomplishments, but bring out the ticker tape parade in celebration of the child.

Bob and his mother never had a very good relationship to begin with. Her words were sharply pointed. However, that comment cut so deep, he never spent much time with her again. Visits were fewer. Phone calls were nonexistent. Twenty years had passed when Bob told me this story, but the pain etched on his face was as though it had happened the day before. "Words will never hurt me?" Nothing could be further from the truth.

Meghan understands Bob's disappointment. All her life she longed to hear her mother say, "Meghan, you are so beautiful!" While she never heard them as a child, it was her wedding day when she thought her dream would come true. However, as her mother straightened her veil and posed with her daughter dressed in a magnificent beaded wedding gown, the words never came. As if someone forgot to light the candles on a cake, Meghan passed the day without hearing the words her little-girl heart longed to hear.

You might be thinking, as I did, *Well, I'm not that bad. I'd never say something so careless as Bob's mom, and I would certainly tell my daughter she was beautiful.* But I wonder…what would my adult son have to say?

Moms should never pat their own backs for their adult children's accomplishments, but bring out the ticker tape parade in celebration of the child.

DON'T PUT DOWN THOSE POM-POMS QUITE YET

When do we outgrow the need for encouragement? When we outgrow our earthly bodies and sit at Jesus's feet. So until we pass through heaven's doors, every person longs to have someone in his corner to cheer him on. When an adult child gets married, the head cheerleader is the spouse; however, the need for an encouraging, supportive parent is something they never outgrow.

When Ruth's daughter was born, her mother began to tell her about all the travails of raising a girl. In the middle of her advice about navigating the dating years, her mother said, "But I didn't have to worry about that with you because you weren't pretty enough for the boys to be interested."

It was a careless remark made by an insensitive mother. She's gone now, but the wounds of her words linger beyond the grave.

"I don't know what else Mom said after that," Ruth remembered. "My heart stopped on that one sentence and froze there. I still feel the disappointment like it was yesterday. I now understood the reason for so many of my insecurities. All my life my mom had criticized me. Staring down at my perfect baby girl, I made a decision that she would always know that she is a loved, beautiful, amazing creation of God who could accomplish anything she set her mind to. Today that baby girl has a Ph.D. from the University of Washington. I love her deeply. One of my biggest regrets is that I was not able to shield her from her grandmother's caustic remarks. And when she thinks of her grandmother, it is her sharp tongue and demeaning words that she remembers most."

Ruth flipped the flow of discouraging words that drowned out her self-esteem. As a result, her daughter was awash with courage-pumping inspiration to live her best life.

When I asked boomers to tell me ways in which their mothers used their words well once they were an adult, the usual response was silence. They think. They ponder. They take a deep breath. A few of my friends said they couldn't really think of anything. Can I tell you how sad that makes me? It's an unfortunate trick of the mind that the human brain tends to remember negative events more than the positive. Different hemispheres of the brain handle these contrasting emotions, and the negative emotions and events require more thinking, processing, and ruminating.[4] That's why unpleasant events are so deeply engrained in our minds, while the positive ones slip away.

One woman responded to my question, "My mom told me that I made the best dill pickles she had ever eaten." Dill pickles? Really? That was the only encouraging word she could remember from her mother as an adult?

Friend, we can do better than that. Let's use our words wisely so that if someone asked our adult child how his or her mom used her words to encourage, they would say, "My mom has given me so many encouraging words as an adult, I don't even know where to start."

While we aren't to use our words
to necessarily steer the adult child,
we can use our words to steer
the relationship between us.

I BELIEVE IN YOU

Jonathan was a young adult that was trudging through the murky waters of rejection by his father. His dad left the family when Jonathan was in middle school. He had maintained the semblance of a relationship with Jonathan's older brother and sister but had not done so with Jonathan. He and his dad had an argument during Jonathan's second year in college, and his dad never talked to him again. His wounds ran deep and bled long. It seemed that every single part of his life was affected by the abandonment and the feeling of being unlovable by the one person who was supposed to love him no matter what.

But Jonathan had (and still has) an incredible mom. Pat understood the wounds and dressed them with the salves of love, prayer, and encouraging words as best she could. One particular Thanksgiving, Jonathan's father invited Jonathan's two siblings to join him for Thanksgiving. The knife of rejection turned yet another notch. The night before spending the holiday with his mom, Jonathan went to a party of old high school friends. Before he left, Pat, his mom, looked her son in the eye and said, "You call me if you need me for any reason. At any time. I'm here for you."

Jonathan, wrapped in pain, waltzed into the party and went straight for the alcohol. By midnight, he was hugging the toilet, drunker than he'd ever been in his life. At 2:30 a.m. he called his mom to come get him.

"Mom came to the house, gathered me in her arms, and helped me get in the car. I was a mix of alcohol, vomit, and tears. All the while, she rubbed my back and said, 'Oh, buddy. You don't have anything to prove to those people. You don't have anything to prove to anyone. You are so loved. I love you so much. You're going to be okay.'"

Here's what Pat did not do. She didn't fuss at Jonathan and tell him that she was disappointed in him, but comforted Jonathan and told him that she was there for him. She didn't add to his growing list of self-loathing by pointing out his failure, but added to his worth as a child of God by pointing out his great value. She didn't yell at him for making a bad decision by drinking, but praised him for making a good decision by calling her. Ten years later, Jonathan still recalls the moment that his mom picked him up off the floor of rejection with her words.

I asked Jonathan how his mom has continued to use her words in positive ways now that he's in his midthirties, and he quickly answered, "Prayer. By the time I get up in the morning," he said, "my mom is already posting pictures of her open Bible with highlighted verses and prayers that she is offering up for me and my wife. Her words have been the greatest source of encouragement in our married life."

One of the best ways the mother of an adult child can use her words is through prayer. When our children are little, we talk to them about God. When they are grown, we talk to God about them. Consider the words to this poem:

THE WARRIOR

This morning my thoughts traveled along
To a place in my life where days have since gone
Beholding an image of what I used to be
As visions were stirred and God spoke to me.

He showed me a Warrior, a soldier in place
Positioned by Heaven, yet I saw no face
I watched as the Warrior fought enemies
That came from the darkness with destruction for me.

I saw as the Warrior would dry away tears
As all of Heaven's angels hovered so near
I saw many wounds on the Warrior's face
Yet weapons of warfare were firmly in place.

I felt my heart weeping, my eyes held so much
As God let me feel the Warrior's prayer touch
I thought "how familiar," the words that were prayed
The prayers were like lightning that never would fade.

I said to God, "Please, tell me the Warrior's name."
He gave no reply, He chose to refrain
I asked, "Lord, who is broken that they need such prayer?"
He showed me an image of myself standing there.

Bound by confusion, lost and alone
I felt the prayers of the Warrior carry me home
I asked, "Please show me, Lord, this Warrior so true."
I watched and I wept, for Mother…the Warrior was you!

©1993 Larry S. Clark

LET ME HELP YOU...
OR MAYBE NOT

Krista's mom was coming for a visit, and Krista's stomach was already tied in knots. As a child, her mom constantly told her what to do and how to do it. And to top it off, Krista felt she never did it quite good enough. Now she was 33 years old, but she still felt like that 8-year-old little girl when Mom came to visit.

During one of her visits, her mom said, "Krista, I have some extra time today. Would you like for me to rearrange your bookshelves to look better?" What Krista wanted to do was to scream and say, "No! I like them just the way they are! You do your bookshelves the way you like them, and I'll do mine the way I like them! Leave my stuff alone." Instead, she just stuffed her frustration and said, "No, thank you."

Brittany's mom was much the same. On one visit, she pulled Brittany into the bedroom and said, "I want to tell you something." Brittany thought it unusual but was hoping her mom was finally going to share something meaningful for a change. Instead, her mom said, "Brittany, let me show you how to tuck the corners of your sheets in properly." She began to demonstrate the perfect military folds. Brittany just stood there. "Unbelievable," she said as she turned and walked out the door.

Grace was so excited about her newly painted kitchen and window treatments. She loved the gray walls and crisp, cool white of the valance with a hint of blush. But when her mother stopped by, she said, "Why in the world did you paint your walls gray? You need color in this room. But if that's what you like, oh well."

"Mom, I can't believe you said that," Grace cried. "I love it. Why don't you ever pay me one simple compliment?"

"Well, I'm just trying to be helpful," her mom shrugged.

I heard hundreds of stories similar to those, but I think this is enough to give us a good idea of how to have a bad relationship. My mom was like Krista's, and even though Mom has left this earth, I can still feel that knot tied with the cords of frustration in my stomach that came with her visits.

So what's a mom to do? First, know your adult child. If offering to help has been interpreted as interfering in the past or made him or her feel that you thought he or she was incapable, then don't do it. Also, ask yourself, *Do I want to help my adult child be like me and do things like me, or do I want to help relieve pressure on my adult child to accomplish his or her goals?*

Here's what the young adults told me they would rather hear: "You're doing a great job at...I'm here to help if you ever need it. Just let me know."

SILENCE CAN BE DEAFENING

I was interviewing a 30-year-old man about how his mom's words have affected him as an adult. He is an awesome guy who is in his fourth recovery. His parents have done an amazing job at navigating those rough waters. In the interview, I was sharing about the importance of parents keeping their lips zipped, and he brought up such a great point.

"Silence can be just as judgmental as actual words," he began. I was thinking, *Oh no, not another variable!* He went on to explain. "Let's say that the adult child gets a sleeve tattoo (which he had), and when the mom sees it, she just acts like it's not there. Makes no comment at all. Won't even look at his arm. That adult kid knows she's ticked and hates it so much she won't even acknowledge it. That's just as judgmental as if she just said the words."

"Well, if she does hate it," I asked, "what's she supposed to say?"

"She could make a joke about it, such as 'What a lovely skull.' That always lightens the tension. Or she could say, 'I see you got another tattoo. Do you like it? Did it turn out like you'd hoped?' But acting like it's not there isn't the answer."

I remember when Steve and I had a large pastel portrait of my five-year-old son and his dog commissioned. We loved it and hung it over the fireplace (where it still hangs 30 years later). When Steve's mom came in our den after it was in place, she didn't say a word. Acted like it wasn't there. It was the elephant in the room. Obviously, she didn't like it, and her silence made it loud and clear. What could she have said? "I see you got a portrait of Steven done. What pretty colors. I know you'll enjoy that for years to come." So ignoring a difficult situation is not the solution.

Acknowledge the elephant, even if you wish it were in someone else's zoo. But be kind. It's not your elephant anyway.

I WANT TO PROTECT YOU...
OR MAYBE NOT

Cole was a free spirit. He loved tattoos, loud music, and motorcycles. He called his mom just to say hello, but a few minutes into the conversation, he wished he hadn't. "Are you wearing your motorcycle helmet?" she asked. "I know the Florida law doesn't require it, but I worry. You need to put that helmet on your head! Suppose you had an accident!"

That might sound like pretty good advice, but it wasn't necessary. It was actually detrimental. This was the umpteenth time his mom had talked about her concern with the motorcycle helmet. Cole was not going to think to himself, *You know, she's right. I think I'll start wearing my helmet.* On the contrary, he thought, *I am so sick of her talking about the helmet. I wish I hadn't called.*

What would be a better way for Cole's mom to handle the helmet situation? Say it once. It's one thing to tell an adult child that you are concerned about something that could affect his well-being. It is quite another to repeat it again and again. One way to handle that is to preface the comment with this: "Son, I know this is none of my business, but I am really worried about your safety. Are you sure it's a good idea not to wear a helmet when you ride your motorcycle?"

There, you've said it. Now, don't bring it up again. Remember Proverbs 27:15: "A quarrelsome wife is like the dripping of a leaky roof in a rainstorm." We can slide *quarrelsome mom* right in that verse as well. Drip, drip, drip.

Your adult child is not going to change his behavior because you don't like it. He or she will change behavior when they decide it needs to be changed. All the parent does is create a rift in the relationship by bringing it up time and time again. Once you voice your concern, the next time you voice it needs to be with God. And the good news is, He doesn't mind if you bring it up every day!

It is not the parent's role to protect the adult child. Oh, I wish it were. Don't you? But it's not. One thing we can do is pray, pray, pray. When children are little, we talk to them about God. When they are adults, we talk to God about them.

THE WOMAN OF THE HOUSE...
AND IT'S NOT MOM

Once an adult child gets married, there is a new woman of the house...and it's not Mom. Whether it is a son taking a wife, or a daughter taking a husband, the wife is now the queen of her castle. The mother or mother-in-law is a guest.

In the Garden of Eden, after fashioning Eve, God presented her to Adam. Then He said, "Therefore shall a man leave his father and his mother, and shall cleave unto his wife: and they shall be one flesh" (Genesis 2:24 KJV). The English Standard Version translates the word *cleave* as *hold fast* to his wife. The NIV says the man *is united* to his wife.

Cleave is a word we don't use much today. The Hebrew word is *dabaq*, and means "to cling, closely pursue, deeply attracted to, fasten its grip, to hold fast, remain steadfast, stay, stick together."[5] Like gluing two pieces of paper together, the couple is glued in such a way that if anyone were to try to pull them apart, pieces of one would cling to the other.

Leaving doesn't mean that the new couple doesn't have anything to do with their parents anymore. It does mean that the newly formed family of two takes priority over all other earthly relationships. As I put it in my book *Lovestruck,* "Just as a newborn baby cannot exist outside the womb until the cord is cut, a new couple cannot thrive outside the family of origin until the tether that has held them to their mother and father is severed."[6]

When a man defers to his mother rather than his wife, it creates a wedge between him and his wife that God never intended. Likewise, when a wife confides in her mother rather than her husband, she is placing her mother in a position solely reserved for her husband. These are little foxes that can ruin the vineyard. Moms, we should never place the married adult child in a place where he or she has to choose between us and his or her spouse. Keep it zipped. Encourage the adult child to talk to his or her spouse for resolution.

The wife being the queen means that Mom (the guest) doesn't get to tell her how to decorate her house, clean her house, or organize her house. Barb said this about her daughter-in-law: "At first our relationship was tense. But once she figured out that I wasn't going to try to tell her how to decorate or run her home, we were fine. Now we're very close friends."

And remember, even though you might have an open-door policy for their visits to your house, never expect them to have an open-door policy for theirs. Wait to be invited, or ask when is a good time to come by. And never guilt your way into an invitation with words such as, "It's been so long since we've seen you. Don't you miss us?"

If you're holding this book as a mother-in-law, I encourage you to do everything you can to make it easy for your son or daughter to leave and cleave to his or her spouse. Help your adult child live guilt-free when establishing family traditions that might not include you. Watch your words. Encourage your adult child to lean on his or her spouse for advice and support rather than coming to you. Never make your married child feel conscience-stricken for choosing his or her spouse over you. Better yet, never make your married child feel as if he or she *has* to choose at all.

BASIC GUIDELINES FOR LIVING ON THE SIDELINES

As I said earlier, the power of a woman's words to her adult children is complicated. While it's not possible to delve into all the variables and possible scenarios, I'd like to make a list for us of some common dos and don'ts I gleaned from my interviews. I hope you'll find them helpful. As a caveat, these suggestions are for relatively healthy relationships, but don't apply if there is a life-threatening situation.

Words That Make Adult Children Want to Run for the Hills (aka: Don't Say It!)

1. Don't tell them how to raise their children. Those precious little ones are their children, not Grandma's.

2. Don't remind them of the way you raised them, such as "That's not the way I raised you" or "I would have never let you get away with that." Believe me, they got it. If they choose a different route, then that's their decision. This does not mean omitting funny stories about their childhood. Steven loves to tell stories about how we raised him, especially the discipline variety.

3. Don't be rude. Don't allow a family connection to be an excuse for rudeness or lack of respect. Talk to your adult

child with the respect you would any other adult. When speaking to him or her, ask yourself, *Would I speak to a friend that way?* If not, don't say it, or say it in a different way.

4. Don't jump in with solutions and ideas to try to solve his or her problems. Rather, be a sounding board and ask good questions. Allow the adult child to come to his or her own solutions, even if you don't think they are necessarily the best ones.

   It might take every bit of restraint you have in you, but don't give advice unless you're asked for it. Then reply with, "What I would do…" rather than "What you should do." We all know that wisdom comes with age. But here's a question to ponder: Where did that wisdom come from? I don't know about you, but most of my wisdom came from trial and error—mostly error. Once adult children see that the parent is not going to give unsolicited advice, he or she will be more likely to ask for it. If you act like a CEO who is giving directions, rather than a consultant who is helping them work toward a solution or resolution, they will keep their problems to themselves.

5. Never share a private conversation that you've had with your adult child with someone else. This is true for any shared confidence, but it's worth emphasizing in a parent/ adult child relationship.

6. Don't take it personally if the adult child doesn't have time for a long, drawn-out discussion on any particular day. Remember how busy your life was when you were raising kids, and don't take it personally. And just because Mom and Dad have retired and have time on their hands doesn't mean that their adult kids have time to suddenly fill their void.

7. When adult children call on the phone, don't say, "I was wondering when I was going to hear from you" or "I haven't

heard from you in a long time." Avoid any statement that makes him or her feel guilty for not calling earlier.

Relationally Destructive
Statements to Avoid:

- I told you so.

- You should have listened to me.

- Someday you'll see it my way.

- Wait until you have kids. Then you'll understand.

- When are you getting married?

- Your biological clock is ticking. When are you going to give me a grandchild?

- Have you gained weight?

- Have you started exercising yet?

- Have you been going to church?

- Have you been reading your Bible?

- What were you thinking?

- When are you coming to see me again? Rather, consider: Life is busy, isn't it? I look forward to when we can see each other again.

- I raised you better than that.

- Your complexion (hair, nails, clothes) looks bad.

- Do you really like that car (dress, shirt, house, apartment, or anything that they have purchased)?

- You need to be more responsible.

- You don't love me. (Big no-no. This is the atom bomb for the relationship between a parent and adult child.)

*Relationship Building Statements That
Make Adult Kids Want to Hug Your Neck*

- "I'm so proud of you." That is probably the number-one accolade your adult child wants to hear from his or her parent.

- "You're such a great mom (dad). You're doing a great job raising your kids." Praise your child's parenting skills.

- "You're so smart. I would have never thought of that!" Let your adult child be the teacher. For 18 years, your job was to teach the child. Now that the child is an adult, allow him or her to teach you. That will show a great level of respect and trust.

- "I have confidence that you'll make a good decision."

- "Your home is so warm and inviting." Adult children are proud of their homes. Let them know you are too.

- "How did I get such a son/daughter? I always knew you'd be an amazing adult."

- "You are doing such a good job at work. I know they are glad to have you."

- "If you ever need any help, just let me know. I'm here for you."

- "You're making such a difference in the lives of the people you encounter."

- "That's interesting. I've never looked at it that way before." When he or she shares an opposing view, rather than jump in to share your view, affirm theirs.

- "I heard such and such on the news today. What do you think about it?" Have adult conversations about movies, jobs, and world issues. In discussing politics, be careful. Let them know you would like to know their views on various issues, but never say theirs is wrong and yours is right. My son and I have very different political views. One morning having coffee, I asked him why he voted for a certain party. During the conversation I didn't disagree or interrupt. I did say, "I can see how that would be important to you." Then in return, Steven asked, "Why do you vote for your party?" I answered the same, listing what was important to me. Neither one of us disagreed with the other, even though our views are very different.

- Be respectful. Talk to your adult child with the respect you would give your best friend. If not, don't say it, or say it in a different way.

- Think before you speak. This is the rule of thumb for all of our verbal communications. Ask yourself, *How would I feel if my mom said this to me?*

- Become a master listener. When it comes to communicating with your adult child, listening is so important. Listening shows them that we are interested in what they have to say. It tells them that we are willing to learn from them.

- Talk to your adult child as an equal. Never talk down to him or her, as if you're the expert.

- Whether it's daily or weekly, communicate with your adult child regularly. When you've laid the groundwork for a good relationship, it will be easier to tackle difficult conversations.

- Look for common interests or activities and do them together. Then use that as a springboard for fun conversation.

- Find a good time to talk. I know my son doesn't like for me to call or text him during work hours or weekend nights. We've found that he prefers texts if we want to get in touch with him, and he prefers the phone if he wants to get in touch with us. Everyone is different.

- Consider your intentions before you share an opinion that you know is opposed to theirs. Are you sharing your opinion or trying to change someone else's? If you are trying to change someone else's, then it's best to keep quiet.

- If the adult child makes it clear that he or she doesn't want to talk about a certain topic, then don't bring it up. Respect their wishes. They will be more likely to listen to the parent if they feel that the parent has listened to them.

- Be mindful of timing when bringing up sensitive subjects. We all know that there is a time to speak and a time to be silent (Ecclesiastes 3:7). That is true in every facet of life, and we'll look at that in a later chapter. When it comes to talking about a potentially emotionally charged issue, make sure the time is right. You wouldn't want to try to have a serious discussion with your husband during the Super Bowl. Likewise, we need to be aware of broaching certain topics when the adult child is under stress at work, struggling with their marriage, or disappointed or discouraged in life already.

- Listen to yourself. How would you feel if your mother said the same words you are about to say? Consider your words as if you were eavesdropping on someone sitting at a table beside you. Would you be appalled at the mom's words or applaud the way she communicated?

- When listening to an adult child voice a problem or difficult situation, rather than offer your opinion or advice, ask good questions to help him or her come to their own solutions. Such as, "What are the pros and cons if you choose option A?" "What do you think is the best way to handle the situation?" You might be surprised that their solution is much better than what you were thinking. If not, they'll figure it out. However, if they ask your opinion, give it. Consider saying, "What I would do is…" rather than "What I think you should to do is…" If you truly have no idea, don't feel like you have to give a solution because you're the parent. Simply say, "I honestly don't know what I would do, but I will pray that God will give you wisdom and direction."

- Be sensitive to what is important to them. If they fight for animal rights, don't talk about your new mink coat. I don't have a mink coat, and you probably don't either. But I think you get the idea.

- Tell your adult child what you appreciate about him, what you admire about her, or what you have learned from him. Remember back to the chapter on the power of a woman's words to her children. Some things we never outgrow, and one of them is the need for encouragement. Continue to be that grown man's cheerleader! No one likes to be around people who are constantly pointing out their faults and shortcomings. And if that is what the adult child hears, he will stop coming. Constantly pointing out shortcomings will stop the adult child from coming at all.

- Keep phone calls, texts, FaceTime, Marco Polo, or any other forms of communication as positive as possible. Avoid sharing all the negative family news, aches and pains, community problems, or other negative chatter that he or she doesn't need to know about. If the phone call is enjoyable and uplifting, the adult child will be more likely to call.

Especially These

THE POWER OF A WOMAN'S
WORDS TO FELLOW BELIEVERS

The world at its worst needs the church at its best.

Author Unknown

A woman called Butterball Turkey's consumer hotline and asked about the advisability of cooking a turkey that had been in her freezer for 23 years. The customer service representative told her that it might be okay to eat it if the freezer had maintained a below-zero temperature the entire time, but even so the flavor would have deteriorated so much that it wouldn't be very tasty. Then the caller said, "Oh, that's what we thought. We'll just donate it to the church."

Many times we tend to give "leftovers" to the church or fellow brothers and sisters in Christ, but when it comes to encouraging words, Paul tells us believers need them most of all: "As occasion and opportunity open to us, let us do good [morally] to all people [not only being useful or profitable to them, but also doing what is for their spiritual good and advantage]. Be mindful to be a blessing, *especially to those of the household of faith* [those who belong to God's family with you, the believers]" (Galatians 6:10 AMPC). In his letters to the churches of the New Testament, Paul reminded Christians to use their words to build up the body of Christ because he knew how easy it is to tear it down.

A LITTLE APPRECIATION
GOES A LONG WAY

I know this book is about the power of a woman's words, but we can learn a lot about how to use our words to encourage the body of Christ from a burly man—Paul. When I think of Paul, I tend to think of a stoic, stern rock of a guy who is neither swayed nor deterred from the course at hand. I see him needing no one other than Christ Himself. But that was not true! Paul needed the encouragement of other believers. He longed for the words of fellow Christians to cheer him on while spreading the gospel.

Ponder these words he penned to the Corinthian church:

> When we came into Macedonia, we had no rest, but we were harassed at every turn—*conflicts on the outside, fears within.* But God, who comforts the downcast, comforted us by the coming of Titus, and not only by his coming but also by the comfort you had given him. He told us about your longing for me, your deep sorrow, your ardent concern for me, so that my joy was greater than ever (2 Corinthians 7:5-7).

What was Paul feeling at this time? Conflicts on the outside and fears on the inside. Yes, that mighty man of God who said, "I can do all things through Him who strengthens me" (Philippians 4:13 NASB) also struggled with fear, fatigue, and discouragement of the worst kind.

Paul was a spiritually confident man. He wrote: "We are hard pressed on every side, but not crushed; perplexed, but not in despair; persecuted, but not abandoned; struck down, but not destroyed" (2 Corinthians 4:8-9). "Who shall separate us from the love of Christ? Shall trouble or hardship or persecution or famine or nakedness or danger or sword?…No, in all these things we are more than conquerors through him who loved us" (Romans 8:35-37). Paul believed these words with all of his heart, and yet he still needed the words of fellow believers to encourage him to press on.

Even as I write these words, I am struck with just how desperately fellow Christians need encouraging words to continue in the faith. It is easy to say, "Well, God should be enough. People should find their strength in Christ." Yes, Christ is enough for salvation. However, God has placed us in a body—a community of believers. He called us the body of Christ because we are dependent on each other to function well, to love well, to struggle well.

One of my friends, Ann, opened up with me about the disappointment she felt after a women's retreat. "I had worked all year long on the women's retreat," Ann explained. "I didn't get a paycheck, but that wasn't what I was doing it for in the first place. I was planning the retreat to honor Jesus. I'll admit, though, that I longed for someone to tell me, 'I appreciate all your hard work,' or 'You really ministered to me,' or 'Thank you for all you do to encourage women.' I didn't do all that work for a pat on the back, but a pat on the back would have meant so much. I'm not sure I have it in me to do it again."

I wonder if a few positive words of thanks or appreciation would have given Ann the fuel she needed to tackle the women's retreat for another year. While the women who attended were filled, Ann left empty. Take a look at how Paul used his words to encourage the various churches in the New Testament:

> I thank my God every time I remember you. In all my prayers for all of you, I always pray with joy because of your partnership in the gospel from the first day until now, being confident of this, that he who began a good work in you will carry it on to completion until the day of Christ Jesus. It is right for me to feel this way about all of you, since I have you in my heart and, whether I am in chains or defending and confirming the gospel, all of you share in God's grace with me. God can testify how I long for all of you with the affection of Christ Jesus. And this is my prayer: that your love may abound more and more in knowledge and depth of insight, so that you may be able to discern what is best and may be pure and blameless for the day of Christ, filled with the fruit of righteousness that comes through Jesus Christ—to the glory and praise of God (Philippians 1:3-11).

> We always thank God, the Father of our Lord Jesus Christ, when we pray for you, because we have heard of your faith in Christ Jesus and of the love you have for all God's people—the faith and love that spring from the hope that is stored up for you in heaven and about which you have already heard in the true message of the gospel that has come to you. In the same way, the gospel is bearing fruit and growing through-out the whole world—just as it has been doing among you since the day you heard it and truly understood God's grace. You learned it from Epaphras, our dear fellow servant, who is a faithful minister of Christ on our behalf, and who also told us of your love in the Spirit (Colossians 1:3-8).

Now look at Paul's words of encouragement to one particular fellow believer, Timothy:

> I thank God, whom I serve, as my ancestors did, with a clear conscience, as night and day I constantly remember you in my prayers. Recalling your tears, I long to see you, so that I may be filled with joy (2 Timothy 1:3-4).

Simple words, but powerful words. I imagine Timothy, as well as the churches in Philippi and Colossae, read those words time and time again. Not only did Paul show us how to use our words to spur on fellow believers, he reminded others how to use their words as well. He wrote to Timothy, "Set an example for the believers in *speech,* in conduct, in love, in faith and in purity" (1 Timothy 4:12).

HONORING THE BRIDE

I ran into Shelly at the grocery store. She had just returned from a visit with her prospective daughter-in-law. Her son was getting married in a few months, and the weekend was intended to help the two families become better acquainted.

"I will tell you one thing," Shelly began, "she might be a Christian, but there is one chapter in the Bible that girl has not read…Proverbs

31. She doesn't know the first thing about how to be a wife. And I know where she got it from. Her mother. She made all the decisions. It was her show. All weekend it was evident that the women in this family were in charge." Shelly continued pointing out the shortcomings of the bride as I grew more uncomfortable by the minute. My heart went out to her...not to the mother-in-law, but to the bride. I was so glad her son wasn't there to hear it. This young gal had no idea she had been closely scrutinized and come up lacking. It made me a little sick to my stomach.

Then I wondered how God's Son, Jesus, feels when we talk badly about His bride. When we scrutinize and criticize fellow believers who are just as flawed as we are. When we evaluate and expectorate brothers and sisters in Christ as if we're the ones sitting on the judgment seat. Yes, the church has received gut punches from the world around us, but most of the criticism comes from within the family itself.

Jesus knew the propensity of His followers to criticize each other. He also knew the destructive potential of our negative words to turn those on the outside looking in away from the faith. Jesus said, "A new command I give you: Love one another. As I have loved you, so you must love one another. *By this all men will know that you are my disciples, if you love one another*" (John 13:34-35). In Jesus's final words before His arrest, He prayed that we would be unified as one: "My prayer is not for them alone. I pray also for those who will believe in me through their message, that all of them may be one, Father, just as you are in me and I am in you. May they also be in us so that the world may believe that you have sent me" (John 17:20-21).

Did you catch that? "So that the world may believe..." If we use our words against each other rather than for each other, the world will say, "Why would I want to be a part of that?"

Others in the Bible instructed us not to speak ill of the bride. At least 55 times, the words *one another* appear in the Bible. Here are just a few:

> Be devoted to one another in love. Honor one another above yourselves (Romans 12:10).

Live in harmony with one another (Romans 12:16).

Accept one another, then, just as Christ accepted you, in order to bring praise to God (Romans 15:7).

Encourage one another daily, as long as it is called "Today," so that none of you may be hardened by sin's deceitfulness (Hebrews 3:13).

Be completely humble and gentle; be patient, bearing with one another in love (Ephesians 4:2).

Be kind and compassionate to one another, forgiving each other, just as in Christ God forgave you (Ephesians 4:32).

Bear with each other and forgive one another if any of you has a grievance against someone. Forgive as the Lord forgave you (Colossians 3:13).

Encourage one another and build each other up, just as in fact you are doing (1 Thessalonians 5:11).

Did you notice how many of these "one anothers" involved words? God has called us to live in community and to use our words to build unity.

EMPOWERING OTHERS TO DO
WHAT GOD CALLED THEM TO DO

Female leaders in the Bible aren't plentiful, but Deborah's story in the fourth chapter of the book of Judges is enough to make any woman proud. She was a wise woman who used her words well.

Deborah was a prophetess who led Israel during a time when her people were being oppressed by the pagan king of Canaan. Her name meant "bee," and she was a busy bee indeed. She served as counselor, judge, and warrior. Deborah held court under a palm tree, which became known as the palm of Deborah. The *NIV Study Bible* says this about Deborah and her tree: "The Hebrew word for 'honey' refers to both bees' honey and the sweet syrupy juice of dates. Deborah, the Bee, dispensed the sweetness of justice as she held court, not in a city gate where male judges sat, but under the shade of a 'honey' tree."[1]

I just love that! Many times when I am flitting around like a busy bee, my words are not exactly categorized as honey. As a matter of fact, the busier I get, the more tense and terse my words tend to turn. But not Deborah. Her words were pleasant as a honeycomb and sweet to the soul (Proverbs 16:24).

One day Deborah called for Barak, one of the leaders of the Israeli army. God had given her instructions for this mighty warrior, whose name meant "thunderbolt." As he approached the tree, she passed along his marching orders directly from his Commanding Officer... God: "The LORD, the God of Israel, commands you: 'Go, take with you ten thousand men of Naphtali and Zebulun and lead the way to Mount Tabor. I will lure Sisera, the commander of Jabin's army, with his chariots and his troops to the Kishon River and give him into your hands'" (Judges 4:6-7).

Barak cowered at God's command and, like a little boy, he said, "If you go with me, I will go; but if you don't go with me, I won't go" (Judges 4:8).

"Certainly," Deborah said, "I will go with you. But because of the course you are taking, the honor will not be yours, for the LORD will deliver Sisera into the hands of a woman" (Judges 4:9). (Deborah was not talking about herself, but another woman who would play a major role in the enemies' ultimate defeat. See Judges 4:17-24.) Apparently, Barak did not trust in the power of God and insisted that this woman of faith accompany him onto the battlefield.

Deborah reprimanded Barak for his lack of faith, but she did not shame him or step in and do his job for him. She acknowledged that he was the warrior who was to lead the men into battle, and she was the prophetess who was to encourage and inspire. Deborah didn't take the lead, but rather worked with Barak to accomplish God's goals. She accompanied him to the battlefield, and when it came time for the attack, she spurred him on with encouraging words.

"Go! This is the day the LORD has given Sisera into your hands. Has not the LORD gone ahead of you?" (Judges 4:14).

In those days, a king led the way into battle, and the army followed close behind. Deborah assured Barak that the King of the universe was leading the way, and he had only to follow the Lord into victory.

Barak was inspired by this amazing woman. She pumped courage into his fearful heart, and he did indeed follow God into battle. She taught him not to focus on the 900 iron chariots of the opponent, but on the mighty arm of God. That day, the Lord confused Sisera, and Israel easily routed their enemy. Afterward, Deborah and Barak sang a duet celebrating the nation's victory.

What can we learn from the power of Deborah's words? Her encouragement spurred Barak to become all God had called him to be and do what God had fashioned him to do. She not only gave him the gift of encouraging words, but she walked with him to the battlefield as well. Her words not only bolstered Barak's courage, but also that of the entire army. She stayed true to her calling as an encourager and helped Barak stay true to his as a warrior. She didn't try to be a one-woman show but worked with others to fulfill God's purposes. Deborah was a true *ezer* who used her words well. And we can do the same! Isn't it exciting to think that you and I can be the very women that God uses to help His purposes come to fruition in the lives of others? We can use our words to give courage to the fearful, strength to the weary, and verbal applause to the unappreciated. Baraks fill the church. Who knows, you might be just the woman God has called to give him or her the needed push.

WORDS THAT HINDER OTHERS
FROM MOVING FORWARD IN FAITH

I wish every woman in the church could be like Deborah, but alas, we've got some Miriams too. Miriam was the brave little girl who hid among the reeds to watch her baby brother floating in the Nile among the crocodiles and would-be assassins of the Hebrew baby boys. Because the Hebrews were growing too numerous for Pharaoh's comfort, he issued an edict that all Hebrew male babies must be killed as soon as they were born. But Moses's mother had a dream that her son would live. After she could no longer hide the growing babe in the quiet of her cottage, she wove him his own little ark of reeds, covered it with pitch, and set him afloat in the river. I'm sure she was at home praying that someone, anyone, would come along and rescue her son.

Meanwhile, Miriam hid among the reeds to see what would happen. She watched as Pharaoh's daughter spied the basket, heard the infant cry, and ordered her attendants to draw it from the water. "This must be one of the Hebrew babies," she said. Pharaoh's daughter fell in love with the babe, named him Moses, and decided to make him her own son.

Suddenly, Miriam emerged from her hiding place and bravely suggested, "Shall I go and fetch one of the Hebrew women to nurse the baby for you?"

Not only did Moses's mother get to nurse her son and watch him say his first words and toddle his first steps, she was paid handsomely to do so.

Eighty years later, we meet Miriam again. Only this time she is not hiding among the reeds of the Nile, but leading the fleeing Israelites in praise and worship after their escape from Egyptian bondage. Miriam, like Deborah, is also called a prophetess (Exodus 15:20). She used her words to encourage God's people and her musical talents to lead them in song.

But something happened to Miriam along her journey to the Promised Land. She became disgruntled with Moses's leadership and jealous of his calling. Rather than supporting her brother, she began to attack him with her words. Let's watch Miriam as her words became her undoing.

> Miriam and Aaron began to talk against Moses because of his Cushite wife, for he had married a Cushite. "Has the LORD spoken only through Moses?" they asked. "Hasn't he also spoken through us?" And the LORD heard this. (Now Moses was a very humble man, more humble than anyone else on the face of the earth.) At once the LORD said to Moses, Aaron and Miriam, "Come out to the tent of meeting, all three of you." So the three of them went out. Then

the LORD came down in a pillar of cloud; he stood at the entrance to the tent and summoned Aaron and Miriam. When the two of them stepped forward, he said,

Listen to my words: When there is a prophet among you, I, the LORD, reveal myself to them in visions, I speak to them in dreams. But this is not true of my servant Moses; he is faithful in all my house. With him I speak face to face, clearly and not in riddles; he sees the form of the LORD. Why then were you not afraid to speak against my servant Moses? (Numbers 12:1-8).

Those are words that should strike fear into any of us who dare to speak against God's servants—which includes all Christians. We should be *afraid* to speak against God's elect. As Paul wrote, "Who are you to judge someone else's servant? To their own master, servants stand or fall. And they will stand, for the Lord is able to make them stand" (Romans 14:4).

When the cloud from which God spoke to Miriam and Aaron lifted, Miriam was covered in leprosy, and her skin appeared like snow. Moses, even though he was the one being criticized and questioned, prayed for God to heal his sister. Yes, God did heal her leprous skin and her diseased words, but not before she spent seven days in isolation outside the camp. Ultimately, more than one million people's journey came to a halt for one week because of one woman's ill-spoken words. Her grumbling and gossiping impeded the entire group from heading to where God intended them to go.

Have you experienced a similar situation? A situation in which one person's words or a group of people's words brought God's work to a sudden stop? I have. Many times.

All too often the church becomes a breeding ground for grumbling and gossiping. Church members have very specific ideas about how a church should be run: contemporary music versus traditional music, choir robes versus street clothes, seeker-sensitive versus discipleship of believers, pews versus theater seating. Before you know it, preference trumps purpose, and the journey to the Promised Land comes to a screeching halt. God didn't take too kindly to Miriam's grumbling. While she started out whispering about Moses's choice of a wife, that was not really the issue at all. Her problem was jealousy, pure and simple.

Actually, there was nothing "pure" about it. "Has the LORD spoken only through Moses? Hasn't he also spoken through us?" Her jealous words were just as destructive as the leprosy that ate away at her fingers and toes. Why was only Miriam punished and not Aaron? We don't really know for sure, but I imagine she was the principle pot-stirrer, and Aaron happened to be the first one to take a bite.

Let's back up to Numbers 12:3: "Now Moses was a very humble man, more humble than anyone else on the face of the earth." Some theologians suggest that the word *miserable* is a better translation of the Hebrew word than *humble*:

> Ever since Numbers 11:1, one thing after another had gone wrong for Moses. So in 11:14 he cried out to God that he couldn't bear the pressure any longer. He even asked that he might die to be released from the assignment. So get this…Moses is not in a good place emotionally, spiritually, or physically. What he needed was a pat on the back, but he got a knife in his back instead. His sister and brother's bitter words were just too much for him to bear. He was now the most "miserable" man on the earth. He felt incapable, insecure, and inadequate for the calling at hand. Under the pressure to continue he cried out to God saying, "It is too much!" (11:4). "Now the man Moses was exceedingly miserable, more than any man on the face of the earth!"[2]

When someone is bending under the pressure of trying to serve God and please the grumblers, they need cheers, not boos. They need holy pep talks from the team. "You can do it!" "Thank you for serving us!" "You are such a great leader." "I appreciate you!" These are the words that keep men and women moving forward in the faith rather than giving up and going home.

We have a choice. We can be a Deborah, who dispenses encouragement from the honey tree and walks side by side with Christian soldiers into battle. Or we can be a Miriam, who stirs up strife and causes the march to the Promised Land (or wherever God is leading) to come to a complete stop. I want to be a Deborah. I bet you do too, honeybee.

A COOL DRINK OF WATER
FOR THE THIRSTY SOUL

A few years ago, a friend of mine had a significant, time-consuming role in making stage props and decorations for the church Christmas program. She worked for months on white, flowing robes; sparkling, sheer backdrops; and frosted, glittery stage props. The church was transformed into a picturesque, heavenly wonderland that took our imaginations to a different world. Well over 2,000 people viewed the Christmas program and marveled at her handiwork. And what did she receive for all her effort? One note of thanks.

"Of course, I didn't do the work to get accolades or pats on the back," she told me later. "But I read that one note over and over again."

I deeply regret that I did not write that note.

Many times a word of thanks or appreciation is the only reward a fellow believer receives this side of heaven. The writer of Proverbs wrote, "Whoever refreshes others will be refreshed" (Proverbs 11:25). Another wise saying notes, "Do not withhold good from those to whom it is due, when it is in your power to act" (Proverbs 3:27).

I can't tell you how much it means to me when I get an encouraging e-mail. Ministry is hard, and being a writer is lonely. There are many days when I'm sitting alone in my room, just me and my computer, wondering, *Is this doing anybody any good?* And honestly, sometimes I just feel like quitting. But then I get an e-mail from someone whose life has been impacted in some way. One little note can give me the strength I need to make one more lap. That's what we can do for each other in the body of Christ.

We always have the power to offer an encouraging word. I hope we never withhold the verbal cool cup of water from those traveling down the road of faith with us. Mother Teresa said, "Kind words are easy to speak, but their echoes are truly endless."

The prophet Elisha met a woman who understood that God's people need encouragement along their journey. One day as he was passing through the town of Shunem, a wealthy woman urged him to join her and her husband for dinner. During their time together, she discerned that Elisha was a holy man and decided to build a guest room onto their home for him to use when he came through town. She wanted nothing in return...it was just her way of blessing Elisha, of refreshing him with her words and ways.

Elisha was overwhelmed by her generosity and wanted to give a gift to her in return. But when he offered to speak to the king on her behalf, she assured him that she did not want, need, or expect anything for her kindness. Elisha wouldn't take no for an answer and continued to contemplate the perfect hostess gift.

Gehazi, his servant, came up with a splendid idea...a child. "Well, she has no son and her husband is old," Gehazi remarked. Great idea. Elisha called her to the doorway and announced, "About this time next year...you will hold a son in your arms" (2 Kings 4:16). And she did.

I just love to watch people try to "outnice" each other. That's exactly what we see in the story of Elisha and the woman from Shunem. She blessed him. He blessed her more. How wonderful it would be if we used our words to try to "outnice" each other among our brothers and sisters in the church.

Paul wrote, "Let us consider and give attentive, continuous care to watching over one another, studying how we may stir (stimulate and incite) to love and helpful deeds and noble activities" (Hebrews 10:24 AMPC). This was not a flippant command. Notice the action words: *give attentive care, continuous care, watching over, studying how, stimulate, incite.* Notice at the beginning of Paul's exhortation that he instructs us to observe and then to speak. Not every person needs the same word of encouragement. We watch, we pray, and then we speak the specific words that will refresh them most effectively.

LESSONS FROM A PALMETTO
CANOPIED DANCE CLUB

Nestled 50 feet off Highway 17 in Pawley's Island, South Caro-lina, rests C.J.'s Beach Club. For years, Steve and I eyed the clapboard building tucked in the grove of myrtle trees, but it wasn't the sort of place we would tend to visit. One weekend it was just the two of us on a short holiday at the beach, and we were feeling adventurous. Steve turned the car onto the crushed-oyster-shell parking lot of C.J.'s, and we decided to taste the local nightlife of the coastal South.

C.J.'s was a dance club. Now, before you close the book in shock that we would darken the doors of such a place, I want you to stay with me a moment. We grew up doing a dance called "The Shag," which is like an East Coast swing. This was shag night at C.J.'s, and the disc jockey spinning the 45s was about 70 years old and had a striking resemblance to my mother-in-law.

Steve and I felt a bit uncomfortable as we walked through the doors and noted the neon signs advertising various drinks, but we were com-mitted. All eyes turned toward the new couple as we walked across the threshold…there was no turning back. The smell of popcorn laced with cigarette smoke filled the air as middle-aged couples shuffled their feet to old beach music under the spinning disco ball.

We each ordered a Coke and found a seat. It wasn't two minutes before a couple wandered over to our table and sat down.

"Hi, I'm Tom," the fortysomething man said as he extended his hand to Steve. "And this is my wife, Julie."

"Hi," Julie chimed in.

"Hi, Julie. Hi, Tom," we returned.

"We've never seen you here before," Tom continued. "Do you live around here?"

"No, we're from Charlotte. Just down here on vacation," Steve answered. "What about you two? Are you from around here?"

"We live in Georgetown just down the road," Tom replied. "We come up here to shag on Friday nights. Most of the people in here are regulars. We all know each other. Like one big family."

After 20 minutes of conversation, we knew each other's occupations, children's ages, college alma maters, favorite hobbies, and various branches of their family tree.

"See you on the dance floor," Tom called as they said their goodbyes and made their way to the next table to visit. As soon as they walked away, another couple sat down, and the same friendly banter ensued. Then another couple…then another. By the time we left C.J.'s, we felt as though we had been welcomed into the family. We had walked in as wary strangers and walked away as warm friends.

"Y'all come back when you're down this way again," several called out as we made our way to the door.

As we drove away in silence with the sound of oyster shells crunching under our tires, sadness washed over me. "I have been in many churches in my time, but never one that was as welcoming and warm as those folks were tonight," I whispered. "We have a lot to learn." Steve felt the same.

No one said to the men and women in the dance club, "Now turn and greet someone around you." It was simply spontaneous, genuine interest. What is going to attract the world to the church and ultimately a relationship with Jesus Christ? Genuine interest, caring, and concern. More than door-to-door canvassing, modern facilities, or the latest media-savvy services, relationships are the net that brings in a bounty of souls. Like parched, cracked ground opening wide for a drop of rain, spiritually parched men and women are longing for a drop of love to quench their thirsty souls. Will they look for the relief among those who have the living water, or look elsewhere because we just can't seem to get along? Jesus has what people are truly longing for. Many can't define the longing or who put it there. But we know—and we have the privilege of telling them! That's the power of a woman's words.

The Woman in the Checkout Line

THE POWER OF A WOMAN'S WORDS TO THE WORLD

The gospel does not fall from the clouds like rain, by accident,
but is brought by the hands of men to where God has sent it.

JOHN CALVIN

One cold evening during the Christmas season, a little boy was standing out in front of a store window. The little child had no shoes and his clothes were mere rags. A young woman passing by saw the little boy and could read the longing in his pale blue eyes. She took the child by the hand and led him into the store. There she bought him some new shoes and a complete suit of warm clothing.

They came back outside into the street, and the woman said to the child, "Now you can go home and have a very happy holiday."

The little boy looked up at her and asked, "Ma'am, are you God?"

She smiled down at him and replied, "No, son. I'm just one of His children."

The little boy then said, "I knew you had to be some relation."[1]

As we go throughout our busy days, we are continually met with opportunities to impact others with the words we speak. Yes, our words influence family, friends, and fellow believers. But it is the man in front of us in line at the grocery store, the woman at the checkout counter, the waiter in the restaurant, the fellow passenger on the airplane, or the neighbor across the street who might be our special assignment for the day. Those are the people God brings across our paths who may need a word of encouragement most of all.

Jesus was a very busy man. And yet, He was never too busy to offer a kind word to the men and women who crossed His path on a daily basis. He stopped and spoke to the diminutive Zacchaeus, who was perched in a tree to get a better look at the parade of followers. He took a break from His travels to engage in one of His longest recorded conversations with a weary woman with a sullied reputation at a well. He interrupted His schedule to comfort a mother in the funeral procession of her only son. He took time to deliver a demon-possessed man who stood in His way on the shore. He noticed a lame man among many who crowded around the pool of Bethesda waiting for the healing waters to stir. He paused to recognize the brave woman who reached out and touched the hem of his robe for healing. Jesus noticed...and then He offered words and deeds of comfort and concern.

It appears that each of these incidents in Jesus's life was an interruption in His packed schedule, but they were not interruptions at all. Each encounter was a divine appointment from His heavenly Father, who orchestrated the moments of Jesus's days. Could it be that God is sending us out on special assignment each time we cross the thresholds of our homes? I believe so.

DIVINE APPOINTMENTS—
DON'T MISS THEM

Beth was one of my divine appointments. She was the last passenger on the plane, out of patience and out of breath.

"Someone's in my seat," the disheveled young woman complained to the flight attendant.

"This one is empty," I pointed out.

"Thanks," she huffed as she plopped down beside me.

The beautiful young lady was obviously exhausted. She was dressed in skintight jeans and a distracting, low-cut T-shirt. Her flip-flops slid under her feet to reveal a cute tattoo on the top of her right foot. Sunglasses hid something…I wasn't sure what. She looked straight ahead, but I felt that her mind was looking back.

After the plane left the ground, I pulled out a book I was reviewing for an upcoming radio interview. *Put the book down and talk to this girl,* God seemed to say.

Lord, she doesn't want to talk. I can tell by her body language. She's not interested in conversation, I mentally argued.

Put the book down and talk to this girl. (God can be very persistent. Especially when it comes to one of His own.)

All right, all right, all right. I closed the book and turned to the tight-lipped passenger.

"So where are you headed?" I asked.

"Home," she replied.

"Where's home?"

"Right outside of Charlotte," she replied. "It's a small town. I'm sure you've never heard of it."

"Were you in Florida on business or pleasure?" I continued.

"I was visiting my boyfriend," she answered.

Then she took off her sunglasses to reveal red, swollen eyes. She glanced down at the book in my lap. "*Your Scars Are Beautiful to God,*" she read out loud. "That's an interesting topic. I've got lots of scars."

"So do I. That's why I wrote the book."

"You wrote that book?"

"Yep."

For the next hour and a half, she poured out her heart. She had been abandoned by her birth father and sexually abused by several men in her life. She was on this flight home because her boyfriend, who had just come out of a drug rehabilitation center, had "roughed her up." Actually, she was fleeing. My heart broke as this beautiful young girl told me story after story of cruelties that had been done *to* her mingled with bad choices that had been made *through* her. At the moment, her life resembled a hundred-car train wreck with one lone survivor who was in desperate need of emergency care.

As my mind engaged with Beth (not her real name), my spirit communed with God. *What do I do?* I prayed. *So much hurt. So much pain. Pray for her…now.*

"Beth, would you mind if I prayed for you?"

"No," she said with a quiver in her voice. "I'd like that."

I held Beth's hand, and God's sorrow for this girl filled my heart. It wasn't just a "God bless Beth" sort of prayer. I sobbed. It was as if God's pain for this girl I didn't even know was flowing through me.

As God would have it, Beth and I were on the front row of a sparsely filled plane. The only person paying any attention to us was the flight attendant, who sat facing us in her jump seat. I'm not sure, but I think God was working in her heart as well.

When the plane landed, I handed Beth the book, we exchanged e-mails, we embraced one last time. After that encounter, we touched base a few times. Beth continued her journey to find peace and purpose. Her stepfather wrote me a letter expressing his appreciation for taking the time to minister to his "little girl." He wrote: "I had been praying for God to send Beth an angel, and I believe He did."

Well, I'm no angel, that's for sure. But I believe the angels were hovering around us in that plane. That's what happens when we pay attention to those around us, and use our words to give hope, encouragement, and God's love in a very pain-filled world.

THE IMPACT OF ONE SIMPLE COMMENT

Alan Loy McGinnis, in his book *The Friendship Factor,* tells this story about the power of a woman's words to one of his friends, Bruce Larson, on another airplane adventure. Bruce was on his way from New Jersey to New York to speak at a conference. He was exhausted and totally unprepared for the schedule before him, but he planned on working during the flight. He opened his notebook and prayed, "O God, help me. Let me get something down here that will be useful to Your people in Syracuse."

Nothing came to Bruce, and the closer he got to Syracuse, the guiltier he felt about his lack of preparation. But then something happened that changed his attitude. It was the simple words of a flight attendant. Bruce remembers:

> About halfway through the brief flight, a stewardess came down the aisle passing out coffee...As she approached my seat, I heard her exclaim, "Hey! Someone is wearing English Leather aftershave lotion...Who is it?"
>
> Eagerly I waved my hand and announced, "It's me..."
>
> All through the remainder of the flight the stewardess and I maintained a cheerful banter each time she passed my seat...Twenty-five minutes later when the plane prepared to land I realized that my temporary insanity had vanished. Despite the fact that I had failed in every way—in budgeting my time, in preparation, in attitude—everything had changed. I was freshly aware that I loved God and that He loved me in spite of my failure.
>
> What is more, I loved myself and the people around me and the people who were waiting for me in Syracuse... I looked down at the notebook in my lap and found a page full of ideas that could prove useful throughout the weekend.
>
> "God," I mused, "how did this happen?" It was then that I realized that someone had entered my life and turned a key. It was just a small key, turned by a very unlikely person. But the simple act of affirmation, that undeserved and unexpected attention, had got me back into the stream.[2]

We never know when one simple comment can change the course of someone's day. To a cashier, "Your hair sure looks pretty today." To a frazzled mom in the grocery line, "You're doing such a good job." To the postman, "Thank you for being so faithful bringing our mail every day." To the teenage grocery bagger, "I bet your parents are so proud of you." Look for something positive to say to those who tend to blend into the woodwork. You might be just the one to help them stand out among the crowd.

THE NEED TO BE NOTICED

Advertisers are well aware of the need human beings have to belong. They are banking on it. How many times have my eyes filled with tears over a television commercial? A credit-card commercial shows a grown daughter taking her elderly mother back to Italy to discover her roots… "The cost? Priceless." (I cry.) A horse-drawn carriage glides through the snow on its way to a cozy cottage nestled in the trees with smoke swirling in the sky…"Home for the holidays." (I cry.) A young man dressed in a military uniform drops his duffel bag on his unknowing parents' den floor in the wee hours of the morning and starts the coffeemaker. His mother, smelling the aroma, hurries down the stairs and clutches her hands as tears stream down her cheeks at the sight of her soldier home from war. (I cry.)

The tears that form in my eyes prove that these advertisers have tapped into my need to belong. They would have us believe that if we buy their particular product, we will have that same warm, fuzzy feeling of euphoria or ecstatic joy.

But we know the truth. True joy will not be found on the grocery store shelf, the car sales lot, or the department store window. It cannot be bought with the swipe of a credit card or cold, hard cash. People want to feel they are a part of something bigger than themselves and that there is more to this life than accumulated wealth and accomplishments.

We have the power in our words to tell the world about the way, the truth, and the life. We have the power in our words to help change the world one person at a time.

Everyone wants to be noticed, cared for, and loved. How my heart breaks with David's words: "No one cares for my soul" (Psalm 142:4 NKJV). He is crying out during one of the darkest times in his life and felt all alone in his struggle to survive. We might expect to hear those words from the crowded city streets as men and women scurry about in their power suits, off to make the next deal. We wouldn't be surprised to hear those words from a vagrant huddled under a bridge with all his worldly possessions stuffed in a plastic grocery bag. But would we expect it from the person sitting beside us in the church pew, the coworker in the next cubicle, or the mother of three next door?

While flying from the East Coast to the West Coast, I watched an in-flight movie, a cleaned-up version of *What Women Want* starring Mel Gibson. Nick Marshall (played by Mel Gibson) works at an advertising firm with a host of busy men and women bustling about in their own little, self-absorbed worlds. In a strange twist of events, Nick is "electrically altered" when he slips in the bathroom and falls into the bathtub, along with a hair dryer. When he regains consciousness after his shocking experience, he has the ability to hear women's thoughts. With his new perceptive powers, he lands a huge Nike advertising account and wins the heart of the leading lady...of course. But there is one poignant sideline of the plot that grabbed my heart.

In the movie, one young, nondescript woman in Nick's office has thoughts that stopped Nick cold. *What if I just jumped out the window? Would anyone notice? I could be gone for days and no one would notice... until the files started piling up. Then they'd say, "Where's the geek with the glasses who carries the files?"*

No one noticed the errand girl who refused to make eye contact with her fellow employees...except Nick, who could hear her thoughts.

One day the young woman (who we learn is named Erin), doesn't show up for work.

"Where's Erin?" Nick asked as he notices a pile of files sitting on her desk.

"I don't know," someone replies. "She didn't show up for work today."

Fearing the worst, Nick locates Erin's address and dashes out to stop her from ending her life.

Bursting into her apartment, Nick sees a suicide letter lying on the table and his heart sinks. A startled Erin walks into the room.

"Mr. Marshall, what are you doing here?"

"I'm glad I got here before you hurt yourself."

"What makes you think I was going to hurt myself?"

"I just sensed it."

"Really? You sensed it? That's not good."

Then Nick brilliantly changes course. "The real reason I'm here is to offer you a job. You know we got the Nike account, and we were wondering who would be a real spitfire to work on this project..." Nick offers Erin a place on his team and rescues her from feeling invisible—unwanted, unloved, and unimportant.

I'm not suggesting you watch this movie. After all, it was a cleaned-up airline version. However, I am suggesting that you ponder the situation. I believe men and women walk past us every day, just like Erin in this movie, feeling that they have no significant purpose in this world. I know there are many who feel that their sudden disappearance would cause little fanfare or concern. It might be the woman who passes you in the hall at work, the rebellious-looking teen who shuffles by you at the mall, or the businessman dashing to his next appointment. It takes so little to let someone know they are significant and seen. We have the ability to give someone hope by offering a simple word of acknowledgment.

Dr. David Jeremiah wrote, "We are shaped by those who love us or refuse to love us, and by those whom we love or refuse to love."[3] An amazing opportunity is given to each of us as we walk through our day to shape and mold those around us with a simple word of encouragement, acknowledgment, or appreciation. The world is crying out for love—a positive word, a tender touch, a morsel of praise. Sometimes a simple "hello" can be a boost to someone starving to be noticed. Many people are so lonely that any token of attention is an unexpected oasis that refreshes the soul. In *The Four Loves,* C.S. Lewis said, "Our whole being by its very nature is one vast need; incomplete, preparatory, empty yet cluttered, crying out for Him who can untie things that are now knotted together and tie up things that are still dangling loose."[4] How amazing that sometimes God allows us to participate in setting free and binding together through the words we speak.

As we all know, some people are easier to love than others. But you know what helps me get past the irritating personality, the caustic attitude, or the boorish behavior? Just a little bit of memory. When

I reflect over my past and see just how far God has brought me, I am overwhelmed with gratitude. I don't have to imagine what I would have become if Jesus had not rescued me at the age of 14. I was on the brink of some immoral decisions that would have scarred me for the rest of my life. It was only through His grace and mercy that I did not become a statistic. Fyodor Dostoyevsky is reported to have said, "To truly love someone is to see them as God intended."[5] We can do that. We can speak that.

PUTTING THE SAINTS
INTO CIRCULATION

Oliver Cromwell was a political and military leader in Great Britain in the mid-1600s. During his reign, the government began to run low on silver for coins. He sent his men to the local cathedral to see if they could find any precious metals. They reported back: "The only silver we could find is in the statues of the saints standing in the corners."

Cromwell replied, "Good! We'll melt them down and put them into circulation!"[6]

What a splendid idea! Put the saints in circulation! Paul, when writing to the churches, often referred to Christians as "saints." How fitting that we be melted down and put into circulation, dispensing encouraging words like treasured coins into the heart pockets of a hurting world.

I am convinced that a buffet of ministry exists in restaurants. If ever there was a place where the saints are put into circulation, it is at eating establishments. Americans are eating out now more than at any other time in our country's history, so let's take a look at this unlikely mission field. Here are three scenarios to ponder.

Scenario One

The waiter was haughty, harried, and hurried. Our very presence seemed to be an inconvenience to his evening. His body language shouted, "What do you want? I'm in a hurry. Be quick about it. I don't like you, and I don't want to be here." So I decided to try a little experiment.

"You sure are busy tonight," I said as he plopped our drinks on the table.

"Yep."

"I bet you're going to sleep well tonight."

"Yep."

"I've been watching you scurry around from table to table. You're doing a great job."

Then the waiter looked me in the eye for the first time, stood a bit straighter, and unwrinkled his brow.

When he returned to the table, I continued my experiment. "How long have you been working here?" I asked.

"About four months," he replied. "I had been working in the corporate world and needed to get off the treadmill...the rat race. This is a different type of pressure, but I've lost 30 pounds and feel better than I've felt in years. I'm thinking about going to culinary school in the fall."

"That sounds like a wonderful idea," I said. "I bet you'd be great at it."

He smiled and turned away. Someone noticed that he was more than a waiter...he was a person.

The waiter who gave us our tab at the end of the meal was not the same man who had taken our order an hour before. He had on the same clothes, wore the same nametag, and served the same station. But the frustrated, icy waiter who sloshed our iced tea on the table had thawed into a cheerful young man. That's the power of a woman's words.

Scenario Two

The restaurant was bustling with activity. We bowed our heads to pray as the uncomfortable waitress stood to the side holding a basket of bread. We said our "amens," and then she politely placed the basket on the table and scurried away.

It didn't take long before one of the women in our group began to complain. I knew her propensity to grumble and held my breath. The rolls were cold, the meat was tough, the knife had a spot on it, and where was the ketchup anyway! Several times she pestered the waitress with her nitpicky criticism. I wished we had not prayed. I didn't want anyone observing this woman's critical spirit to know we were representatives of Jesus Christ.

We can all do Jesus a favor. The next time we go out to eat, whether it is at McDonald's or Morton's of Chicago, let's represent Jesus well. We can use our words to make those around us hungry and thirsty to know the hope that is within us. May our compliments flow and grateful spirits nurture their souls.

Scenario Three

I called our waitress over to our table. "Excuse me," I began. "Could I please see the manager?"

"Of course," she nervously replied.

In a few moments, the manager came over to the table. "Is there a problem?" he asked.

"Not at all," I answered. "I just wanted to tell you what a marvelous job Missy did taking care of us today. She is a wonderful waitress, and I hope we have the pleasure of having her wait on us again next time. I just thought you should know what a great job she did and what a treasure you have."

"Thank you, ma'am."

Missy came back to the table beaming. No doubt the manager had relayed our praise. It only took a minute, and those words meant much more to Missy than a 20 percent tip.

Now, let's chew on these three scenarios and digest the ramifications of each. At which table do you see yourself? Which table would you like to join?

GOD'S LIVING LETTERS

I received a letter the other day. It didn't have a stamp in the right-hand corner or even a return address sticker, but I knew exactly where it came from, and there was no doubt as to who had sent it. The letter was wearing jeans and a sweatshirt with brown, shoulder-length hair, and she was sent by God.

In the Bible, Paul described Christians as living letters known and read by everybody, not written with ink, but with the Spirit of God on human hearts (2 Corinthians 3:2-3). God has sent many love letters my way…hand delivered, special delivery, postage paid. Admittedly, some of the letters seem to have become marred in transit, and I suspect a few of the words were not quite what the Author intended. But they were letters nonetheless.

God did not write His letters on fragile sheets of paper or on tablets of stone. He wrote His letters on human hearts for all the world to read. There are some letters that I've received and wanted to mark RETURN TO SENDER across the top. I didn't want the letter and, honestly, I wasn't sure where it came from. It couldn't possibly be from God. The words were harsh, and I suspected they were also counterfeit. Not really from God at all…even though the letter said they were.

Then there are other letters I have received that were so beautifully scripted that I take them out and read them over and over again. They are treasures I hold dear. I read them often, clutch them to my heart, and even place a kiss upon the seal from time to time. These are my favorite letters. They come in all shapes and sizes, but the return address is always evident, even if it has faded with years or rubbed off with wear. I love these letters. God has sent me so many over the years.

Dear friend, here is a daunting thought. You are a letter. I am a letter. God has written His message on our hearts and mailed us out to the world. People read His letters in our actions. They read His letters in our words. What will they read in your letter? Will they welcome the words like a soldier hungry for news from home, or view them like junk mail to be tossed in the trash? Will they dread the words and see them like a bill that needs to be paid, or will they see them as God intended… loving words wooing them to Christ?

A LOST LITTLE GIRL FINDS HOME

Once there was a little girl who grew up in a very nice neighborhood with 60-foot pine trees that shaded a Southern ranch-style home. Her life consisted of a smattering of friends who roamed from house to house; barefoot, hot summer days; and a collie named Lassie who followed her every move. But behind the doors of her house was a family secret. Her father, a businessman in the community, had a drinking problem. Many nights this little girl climbed in bed to the sound of her parents yelling, fighting, and crashing furniture. No one knew what was happening behind the beautiful brick walls and welcoming door.

But there was a woman in her neighborhood, the mother of this little girl's best friend. She loved this little girl and shared Jesus Christ with her. She listened to her troubles, embraced her little frame, and made her feel as though she was extremely loved by God. Their relationship, this bond between a lost little girl and a borrowed mom, continued to grow. Then one day, Mrs. Henderson asked this 14-year-old teen if she was ready to accept Jesus Christ as her Lord and Savior.

The little girl said yes.

The little girl was me.

I am the product of the power of a woman's words. Mrs. Henderson's words to me about Jesus Christ's sacrifice and God the Father's love changed my life. But it wasn't just her words about Jesus that made the difference. It was her words about life in general that drew me like iron shavings to a magnet. She made me want what she had—excitement, enthusiasm, and a zest for life.

Most people are not drawn to Jesus because of an advertising campaign, a sign along the road, or a steeple along the skyline. Most people are drawn to Christ through cords of kindness formed in relationships with other people.

We have the power in our words to make people thirsty to know Christ. It doesn't necessarily come through preaching. It comes through loving, listening, and learning. "How beautiful are the feet of those who bring good news!" (Romans 10:15). That's the power of a woman's words to the world.

Simple Words of Kindness

- Compliment service workers.
- Say "Thank you."

- Show interest and concern when someone appears to be having a bad day.

- Ask questions about someone's interests: "I see you are buying a wedding present. Is it for someone close to you?"

- Greet your neighbors.

- Learn your neighbors' names, and write them encouraging notes during difficult times.

- Find something positive to say to the cashier at the checkout line.

- Start a conversation with the person beside you on a bus, in an airplane, or in line at the post office.

- Offer to help someone. For example, you see a woman struggling with her packages and the baby stroller all at the same time. A simple, "Here, let me help you with that," could be just the words to brighten her day.

- When you see an embarrassed young mother with a child acting up, encourage her with kind words such as, "You're doing a great job" or "Mine did the same thing when he was little."

- Speak kindly to the kids in the neighborhood. So many adults talk down to kids; they'll think you're the greatest!

PART THREE

The Purposeful Pursuit of Taming the Tongue

You're Not in This Alone

Before Pentecost the disciples found it hard to do easy things;
after Pentecost they found it easy to do hard things.

A.J. GORDON

t was a daunting scene. More than 1,200 miles of Alaskan shoreline was covered with black, slimy crude oil, more than 1,000 bodies of once bustling sea otters were littering the coast, and more than
100,000 grounded birds were gasping for air. The *Exxon Valdez* oil spill
dumped 11 million gallons of crude oil into Prince William Sound and
disrupted the ecological balance of nature. Many of its most beautiful
inhabitants, including 150 bald eagles, were killed. The once glacier-
fed waters teeming with life became an oily death trap.

Just as toxins in nuclear waste facilities, city dumps, and industrial
accidents wreak havoc on the environment, toxic words cause destruction to the hearts and souls of people. Paul wrote, "Let no foul or pol-
luting language…[ever] come out of your mouth" (Ephesians 4:29
AMPC). Perhaps as you've read the previous chapters you've cringed at
words you've spoken and wish you could take them back. Words that
have polluted the ones you hold dear. Can we clean up the mess and
repair the damage? Absolutely! We can choose to clean up the verbal
pollutants and break the patterns of toxic words.

All through this book, we've seen examples of how women have used their words in positive, life-giving ways, and negative, heart-breaking ways. Think of our words as a pendulum that swings between those two points. However, I don't want to be a powerless woman who vacillates between the two depending on what mood I'm in on any given day. I want to be a woman who is intentional—who guards her words with the God-given power of the Holy Spirit. And I'm sure you do too. Let's look at five steps to controlling the tongue.

RELY ON THE HOLY SPIRIT

Tongues...most animals have one. Some snakes have forked tongues. Lizards smell with their tongues. Some fish, such as salmon and trout, have teeth on their tongues. Frogs and toads have tongues that whip out at incredible speeds to catch flies and other insects. Their cousin, the chameleon, has a tongue that is as long as its body. An anteater's tongue can stretch to the height of a two-year-old. A gecko uses its tongue to wipe across its eyes like a windshield, and a giraffe uses its 20-inch tongue to clean its ears. The tongue of a blue whale is about the size and weight of a full-grown African elephant.

Even though a human tongue cannot smell out dinner, reel in the catch of the day, or reach to the tops of trees to pick fruit, it can do something even more amazing. The human tongue can create words. Words are an incredible gift, and as we have seen, they have the potential for good or evil. How do we harness such energy and ensure that it is only used for good? Unfortunately, James tells us it is impossible.

"All kinds of animals, birds, reptiles and sea creatures are being tamed and have been tamed by mankind, but no human being can tame the tongue" (James 3:7-8). That's the bad news. Now, here's the good news. While no human being can tame the tongue...God can. It may be impossible for James, and for you and for me, but it is not impossible for God. "Is anything too hard for the Lord?" God asked Abraham after announcing that Sarah's 90-year-old body was going to bear a child (Genesis 18:14).

When we come to faith in Jesus Christ, God gives us the gift of the Holy Spirit. The Holy Spirit is the third person of the Trinity who enables us to do all that God has called us to do. He gives us the power to change!

Jesus explained to the disciples: "You will receive power when the Holy Spirit comes on you; and you will be my witnesses in Jerusalem, and in all Judea and Samaria, and to the ends of the earth" (Acts 1:8). After Jesus's ascension into heaven, the disciples waited for the Holy Spirit as Jesus had instructed.

> When the day of Pentecost came, they were all together in one place. Suddenly, a sound like the blowing of a violent wind came from heaven and filled the whole house where they were sitting. They saw what seemed to be tongues of fire that separated and came to rest on each of them. All of them were filled with the Holy Spirit and began to speak in other tongues as the Spirit enabled them (Acts 2:1-4).

Isn't it interesting that the first manifestation of the power of the Holy Spirit was words and the first visual manifestation was tongues of fire? The disciples were able to speak in the various languages of the men and women who were visiting Jerusalem to celebrate Pentecost. The travelers heard the gospel in their own languages! Yes, that was astonishing. But even more amazing was the courage that arose in the cowardly disciples.

Just a short time before Pentecost, Peter had been so afraid that he denied he even knew who Jesus was. A mere servant girl's question had Peter shaking in his sandaled feet and swearing he was no friend of Jesus. But after being filled with the Holy Spirit, Peter stood up, raised his voice, and addressed the crowd with such a mighty sermon that 3,000 men and women accepted Jesus as their Savior and were baptized. That's what the Holy Spirit can do for timid souls who believe. He can transform a cursing tongue into a confessing tongue.

It is only through the power of the Holy Spirit that we are able to control this little muscle that rests between our teeth. However, change requires cooperation. We must work in tandem with the Holy Spirit to rein in this feisty force. The Holy Spirit gives us the power, but our responsibility is to put God-given principles into practice.

Holocaust survivor Corrie ten Boom spent the last years of her life speaking to men and women all around the world about the God who sustained her during her imprisonment and who delivered her from the Nazi prison camps. During one of her presentations, she held up a lady's white glove.

"What can this white glove do?" she asked. Then she went on to explain…The glove can do nothing.

> Oh, but if my hand is in the glove, it can do many things… cook, play the piano, write. Well, you say that is not the glove but the hand in the glove that does it. Yes, that is so. I tell you that we are nothing but gloves. The hand in the glove is the Holy Spirit of God. Can the glove do something if it is very near the hand? No! The glove must be filled with the hand to do the work. That is exactly the same for us: We must be filled with the Holy Spirit to do the work God has for us to do.[1]

You and I have that power. It's up to us to access it. Remember, the power of the Holy Spirit can do more on our worst days than we can do on our best days. We would be foolish to think that we could control our tongues in our own strength. I'm so glad we don't have to.

The power of the Holy Spirit can do more on our worst days than we can do on our best days.

EXAMINE THE HEART

Have you ever had words fly out of your mouth and then grievously thought, *Where did* that *come from?* Boy, I have. I've flown off the handle rather than get a handle on my words. I've fired a snarky comment when I should have holstered my tongue. I've thrown up and thrown out some words that came from a place I thought I'd cleaned out long ago. But then God reminds me that just because I cleaned my house on Saturday does not mean that I never have to clean it again. And just because I cleaned my mouth out once does not mean that it will stay clean forever. I have to go back to my words' place of origin time and time again with daily maintenance and repair. And where is that place of origin? My heart.

One day some Pharisees and teachers of the law came to ask Jesus about some of His personal and religious practices— especially what He ate and when He washed His hands. Jesus called the listening crowd together and taught them about what's really important—truth over tradition. "Jesus called the crowd to him and said, 'Listen and understand. What goes into someone's mouth does not defile them, but what comes out of their mouth, that is what defiles them'" (Matthew 15:10-11). Jesus continually pointed out the condition of the Pharisees' hearts. They clung to outward religious practices, but what God desired most—their hearts—were hardened and cold.

God love Peter. Peter wanted a little more explanation, so he asked Jesus what He meant.

> "Are you still so dull?" Jesus asked them. "Don't you see that whatever enters the mouth goes into the stomach and then out of the body? But the things that come out of a person's mouth come from the heart, and these defile them. For out of the heart come evil thoughts—murder, adultery, sexual immorality, theft, false testimony, slander. These are what defile a person; but eating with unwashed hands does not defile them" (Matthew 15:16-20).

Here's a big truth: Where something comes out is not where it started. Where the water comes out of the hose is not where it started. Where waste comes out of your body is not where it started. (Sorry for the image. Not my fault.) Where words come out of your mouth is not where they started. They start in the heart.

If we don't address the issue of the heart and skip over to trying to fix our words that come out of it, we'll keep mopping the kitchen floor rather than fix the busted pipe causing the mess in the first place. Anger, grumbling, and gossiping all have their genesis in the heart and mind before they tumble past our lips, so let's start there.

The word *heart* that is used in this passage is from the Greek word *kardia*. It is not referring to the blood-pumping muscle in the chest cavity, but to our thoughts, motives, feelings; our will; and our character. The *kardia* is the seat of our emotions and represents the inner person. The words that escape our lips reveal the condition of our inner man.

Hand sanitizers are available in every scent imaginable. Heaven help us if we get a germ from the shopping buggy or a door handle. Have you ever had someone shake your hand and then walk away squirting sanitizer in his or her palms? I have. I'm not so sure how I feel about that. But don't you wish there was a heart sanitizer? A few squirts and voila, we're good to go. Unfortunately, it's not quite that simple.

All through the Bible we have accounts of God sending men and women out into the world with a message. Whether it is a message of repentance, judgment, deliverance, or hope, God made sure the messengers were placed in strategic moments in time to make an impact on those around them. But God didn't send the messengers out unprepared. He trained them as only He can do, and He always put them through a process to examine their own hearts.

Isaiah was called to prophesy to Jerusalem 740 years before Christ. In the first five chapters, the overriding theme is impending judgment:

> Woe to you who add house to house and join field to field… Woe to those who rise early in the morning to run after their drinks…Woe to those who draw sin along with cords of deceit, and wickedness as with cart ropes…Woe to those who call evil good and good evil…Woe to those who are wise in their own eyes and clever in their own sight. Woe to those who are heroes at drinking wine and champions at mixing drinks (Isaiah 5:8,11,18,20-22).

But then something happens to Isaiah as he sees his own life reflected in God's magnificent glory.

Isaiah had a vision.

I saw the Lord, high and exalted, seated on a throne, and the train of his robe filled the temple. Above him were seraphim, each with six wings: With two wings they covered their faces, with two they covered their feet, and with two they were flying. And they were calling to one another: "Holy, holy, holy is the Lord Almighty; the whole earth is full of his glory." At the sound of their voices the doorposts and thresholds shook and the temple was filled with smoke. "Woe to me!" I cried. "I am ruined! For I am a man of unclean lips, and I live among a people of unclean lips, and my eyes have seen the King, the Lord Almighty" (Isaiah 6:1-5).

I imagine Isaiah was feeling pretty good about himself, being called by God to prophesy to this irksome people. But just when he got out the sixth woe, God decided to hold up the mirror of His holiness in which Isaiah saw his own sin and examined his own heart. And where did the sin manifest itself? His words.

God doesn't convict us of our sin to condemn us. He reveals our sin to clean us. Just as Isaiah was lamenting his foul tongue, one of the seraphim (brightly shimmering, heavenly beings whose name means "burning ones") picked up a live coal with tongs from the altar of atonement and touched it to the prophet's lips. Just as God sent the Holy Spirit to the believers at Pentecost in the form of flaming tongues, He sent the power of the Holy Spirit to cleanse Isaiah's tongue in the form of a fiery coal. The heavenly being touched Isaiah's tongue with the burning coal and then announced that his guilt was taken away.

Now Isaiah was ready to go out into the world and proclaim God's message to His people, and his "Woe is me" was transformed into "Here am I. Send me!" (Isaiah 6:8). Now his heart was right before God.

Isaiah didn't need to change his eating or drinking habits. He didn't need to alter his outward appearance or take extra classes at the local seminary. He needed to have his words purified and his heart fortified so God could be properly glorified. While it is the Holy Spirit that gives us the power to change the words we speak, the desire to change begins in the heart. The Bible says:

Make a tree good and its fruit will be good, or make a tree bad and its fruit will be bad, for a tree is recognized by its fruit...For the mouth speaks what the heart is full of. A good man brings good things out of the good stored up in him, and an evil man brings evil things out of the evil stored up in him. But I tell you that everyone will have to give account on the day of judgment for every empty word they have spoken. For by your words you will be acquitted, and by your words you will condemned (Matthew 12:33-37).

Remember the children's song:

I'm a little teapot short and stout,
Here is my handle, here is my spout.
When I get all steamed up, hear me shout,
Just tip me over and pour me out.

Well, I don't know about you, but when I get all steamed up, what comes out of my mouth isn't always a cup of tea! It's in those unguarded moments of frustration, anger, or pain that our mouths tend to spew out what is really inside.

In the book of Isaiah, the prophet used the example of the people's speech to point to their condition: "Everyone is ungodly and wicked, every mouth speaks folly" (Isaiah 9:17). The lips are the crack from which the condition of the heart seeps.

We cannot act differently from what we believe. Therefore, if we want to change the way we speak, we must examine our hearts. It takes more than washing our mouths with soap to become a woman of clean lips. In the Old Testament, God spoke about the transforming power that would be available to His people through Jesus Christ: "I will give them an undivided heart and put a new spirit in them; I will remove from them their heart of stone and give them a heart of flesh. Then they will follow my decrees and be careful to keep my laws. They will be my people, and I will be their God" (Ezekiel 11:19-20).

The book of Proverbs has much to say about how the condition of our hearts affects our speech:

- Above all else, guard your *heart,* for everything you do flows from it (Proverbs 4:23).

- The wise in *heart* accept commands, but a *chattering* fool comes to ruin (Proverbs 10:8).

- The prudent keep their knowledge to themselves, but the fool's *heart* blurts out folly (Proverbs 12:23).

- Anxiety weighs down the *heart,* but a kind *word* cheers it up (Proverbs 12:25).

- The discerning *heart* seeks knowledge, but the *mouth* of a fool feeds on folly (Proverbs 15:14).

- The *heart* of the righteous weighs its answers, but the *mouth* of the wicked gushes evil (Proverbs 15:28).

- Light in a messenger's eyes brings joy to the *heart,* and *good news* gives health to the bones (Proverbs 15:30).

- The wise in *heart* are called discerning, and *gracious words* promote instruction (Proverbs 16:21).

- The *hearts* of the wise make their *mouths* prudent, and their *lips* promote instruction (Proverbs 16:23).

- One who loves a pure *heart* and who *speaks* with grace will have the king for a friend (Proverbs 22:11).

- Like a coating of silver dross on earthenware are fervent *lips* with an evil *heart* (Proverbs 26:23).

- Enemies disguise themselves with their *lips,* but in their *hearts* they harbor deceit. Though their speech is charming, do not believe them, for seven abominations fill their hearts (Proverbs 26:24-25).

I've noticed that when I haven't been spending enough time with God reading my Bible and praying, then my heart grows musty and my words grow crusty. The key to keeping the heart clean is daily inspection and regular maintenance. We can pray this with David every day:

> Create in me a clean heart, O God, and renew a steadfast spirit within me (Psalm 51:10 ESV).

If we don't address the issue of the heart and skip over to trying to fix our words that come out of it, we'll keep mopping the kitchen floor rather than fix the busted pipe causing the mess in the first place.

RENEW THE MIND

Let's go back to that question, *Where did that come from?* Yes, words start in our hearts, but they also pass through our minds before they escape through our mouths. The problem is, the flow happens so quickly that it seems like a nanosecond fluid motion. The key is to slow down and think before our words are set free to roam the earth.

Have you ever been to a rodeo and watched a lassoing contest? The little calf bursts from the stall, and then the cowboy and his steed follow in close pursuit. With his lasso in hand, the cowboy swings the rope in the air and attempts to catch the little heifer before she escapes out the corral door at the opposite side of the arena. That is a vivid picture of what we must do with the words that attempt to escape the gate (the mouth). We need to lasso them with the word of truth and rein them in. Throw them down in the dirt, and tie them up if necessary.

The Bible teaches us to take every thought captive and make it obedient to Christ (2 Corinthians 10:3-5). Once we lasso a thought (take it captive), we can decide which words leave the gate and which words need to be tied up and secured.

Various studies show that we speak at about 120 to 160 words a minute.[2] That's a lot of little heifers to rope in, but I believe we can do it! Let's take a look at how to reign in our words. First, a thought bursts from the stall called the brain. It runs across the mind, headed for the door called the mouth. In a split second, we must determine if that thought is true, helpful, inspiring, necessary, and kind. You can remember that with the acronym THINK:

T rue

H elpful

I nspiring

N ecessary

K ind

If we determine that the words don't fit that description, then we lasso them with the rope of kindness and never let them out of the gate. If they do line up *true, helpful, inspiring, necessary,* and *kind,* we let them go free.

Toxic thoughts produce toxic talk. Think about what you're thinking about. If you're stewing on toxic thoughts in your head, then you'll be spewing toxic words from your mouth.

Paul gives us a way to detoxify our thoughts by filtering them through the sieve of the truth.

> Whatever is true, whatever is noble, whatever is right, whatever is pure, whatever is lovely, whatever is admirable—if anything is excellent or praiseworthy—think about such things. Whatever you have learned or received or heard from me, or seen in me— put it into practice. And the God of peace will be with you (Philippians 4:8-9).

Much like the acronym THINK, we should consider this about our words:

Are they true? Are these words reliable, certain, in accordance with fact, exact, and accurate? Do they line up with God's truth? For example, when we speak negatively about someone, we should consider: Do these words fit with God's view of this person as His image bearer?

Are they noble? Because I am a child of the King, my words should reflect nobility. Is what I am about to say demonstrating high moral character or ideals? Is it language that exhibits excellent qualities or a person with royal rank?

Are they right? Are these words virtuous, in accordance with fact and not assumption? Are they appropriate, suitable, and reputable? Right words at the wrong time become wrong words. Is this the right time, or do I need to wait for a more appropriate time?

Are they pure? Are these words free from anything that taints or infects the reputation of another? Are these words tainted by my own sin, or do they reflect the righteousness of Christ that has been given to me?

Are they lovely? Do these words inspire love, affection, or admiration? Are they morally or spiritually attractive or gracious? Do these words conjure up a picture of beauty or loveliness?

Are they admirable? Do these words inspire others to see excellent qualities in another person? Do the words paint a picture of praise or excellence?

Are they excellent? Do these words reflect goodness, exceptional merit, or virtue? Are they of a high moral nature? Would God rank them as "excellent" if they were spoken?

Are they praiseworthy? Do these words stir a sense of praise or condemnation?

Now, that is a lot to think about, considering we speak an estimate of 120 to 180 words per minute. It is unlikely that we will have the time or the wherewithal to filter every word through this eight-layer sieve. However, Paul doesn't just leave us with the qualifying list; he gives us the means by which to implement it. "Whatever you have learned or received or heard from me, or seen in me—*put it into practice.*"

It takes practice! Practice! Practice! Practice! (We're going to look at that in a moment.)

But look at the result: "And the God of peace will be with you."

The King James Version of 2 Corinthians 10:5 says it this way: "*Casting down* imaginations, and every high thing that exalteth itself against the knowledge of God, and bringing into captivity every thought to the obedience of Christ." I like that picture of casting down. Once the cowboy slips the lasso around the calf's neck, he throws her to the ground and whips that rope around her kicking legs to make sure the little heifer's not going anywhere. Likewise, we need to cast down those thoughts back to the dirt where they came from and make sure *they* aren't going anywhere.

While we've got the picture of cowboys and cattle in our minds, let's go back to James 3 and look at another animal in the corral—the horse. Paul compares the tongue to a bridle in a horse's mouth: "When we put bits into the mouths of horses to make them obey us, we can turn the whole animal…Likewise, the tongue is a small part of the body, but it makes great boasts" (James 3:3,5). Our words, like a bit in a horse's mouth, can control the course we travel. They can pull us to the left or the right…all depending on who is holding the reins to which the bit is attached.

When I was young, I loved reading the story of a stately steed named Black Beauty. In my early teens, I enjoyed visiting my friend Cammie and riding horses on her parents' dairy farm. We often clicked our heels and raced through the fields laughing all the way.

The horse is a powerful animal, yet with the tug of the reins or the tap of a heel, he will submit to his master's bidding. On the other hand, a wild stallion that has not been brought under control of a master is of very little use. He does what he wants to, and no one wants to ride him.

In the Bible, we are instructed to have a spirit of gentleness, which tempers the words we speak (Galatians 5:23). The Greek word for *gentleness* is *prautes* and suggests a wild horse that has been tamed. Unfortunately, in our modern society, the word *gentleness* connotes being weak. However, the Greek word means anything but weak. Picture a muscular steed, proudly holding his head, poised to move with speed and power, nostrils flaring, but at the same time under his master's control. That is a true picture of *prautes*—gentleness.

The same word, *prautes,* is translated *meek* in the King James Version. When Jesus said He was "meek and lowly in heart" (Matthew

11:29 KJV), He was saying He was submitted to God—mightily powerful but under God's control. Only when we submit our tongues to God will we have the ability to use our words for good. Meekness isn't weakness; it's power under control. It's taming and training our tongues to be under the submission and control of the Holy Spirit.

Let me give you an example. Oh, I hate to admit this, but I fear many will relate—the dents in my armor attest to it.

Before I became a Christian, I was "gifted" with a quick, sarcastic wit. Have you ever been in an argument and two hours later thought of a great comeback or slamming remark? Not me. I could think of them on the spot. I was good—so good. Why, I could have opened up a side business feeding disgruntled wives, employees, and friends quick comebacks through earphones during confrontations. However, after I accepted Christ as my Savior, it didn't take the Holy Spirit long to convict me that my tongue was not glorifying God. Sure, it brought some laughs, but Jesus wasn't smiling. So I began the arduous task of taming my tongue. It was hard letting all those good, sarcastic comments go to waste, but I knew they needed to be lassoed.

I don't want you to think I don't ever have those thoughts anymore. Quite the contrary. I can still hear those comebacks in my head. On many occasions, when someone is telling me about a confrontation with a family member or a coworker, those comebacks still pop up in my mind. When a store clerk makes a snide remark, I can usually think of one snider. So where's the victory? The victory comes when I choose not to let the words out of my mouth. When I lasso the words before they have a chance to run out of the gate. When I offer blessings rather than cursing. When I put on the humility of Christ and take the comments without the retaliation. That, my friend, is choosing to walk in the Spirit instead of choosing to walk in the flesh. It can only happen by the power of the Holy Spirit and becomes easier with practice.

Meekness isn't weakness;
it's power under control.

RETRAIN OUR REFLEXES

Have you ever heard anyone say, "It was just a knee-jerk reaction"? It's like when the doctor taps on your knee and your foot goes flying in the air. You just can't help it.

A verbal knee-jerk reaction or response is a result of habit rather than careful consideration, and you *can* help it. But it's not easy. Reflexes are hard to train.

One day I was driving home from the beach in July 4 holiday traffic. It was Southern muggy hot, and cars were a throng of metal on wheels. Everyone was going faster than the posted speed limit, and I was trying to keep up. I was also young and distracted. Okay, here's the truth: I had just broken up with my boyfriend and was crying my eyes out.

At one point, I felt my front right tire slip off the asphalt and onto the gravel shoulder of the road. In a flood of panic, I heard the voice of my driver's ed teacher from four years earlier: "If you run off the road, do not, and I repeat, do not jerk your car back on the road. Slow down to a stop and then gently guide the car back onto the road."

My mind knew the rule. I was even repeating, "Do not jerk the car, do not jerk the car." Then I promptly jerked the car. I pulled the steering wheel to the left, jerked the car onto the road, and lost control. First the car flew across two lanes of traffic to the left, and then, after overcorrecting again, flew back off the road to the right. As if in slow motion, the car began a descent down an embankment. The weight of the car became unbalanced and began to roll. As the car somersaulted down the embankment, my body tossed and tumbled like a rag doll, bouncing around the car's interior. I wasn't wearing my seat belt. When the car landed upside down at the bottom of the embankment, I was sitting on the ceiling of the passenger's side.

Travelers watched with mouths aghast as the scenario played out before them. You can imagine how amazed they were to see me crawl out of the smashed car's opened window without a scratch. I knew, without a doubt, that I should not have lived through that accident. It was only by the grace of God that I survived.

Thinking back on the day God spared my life, I am reminded how powerful reflexes are. When the car veered off the road, I knew not to jerk the steering wheel, but I did it anyway.

When it comes to changing the way we speak, we may have some very powerful reflexes to overcome. The Bible tells us that when we come to Christ, we are a new creation (2 Corinthians 5:17). However, no one pushes the delete button to erase the old habit patterns that have been formed over time. The Bible calls them old flesh patterns. They are like ruts in the brain that have been formed by years and years of thinking the same thoughts and repeating the same actions. The only way to replace those ruts is to form new ruts. That comes with practice, training, and reprogramming.

I thought about titling this section "The Pendulum of Choices and Change," because a pendulum swings back and forth. But I want to swing one way, toward speaking life, and stay there. The truth is, sometimes we will swing back the other way.

I want to encourage you not to become discouraged if you make a mistake and use your words negatively from time to time. Satan would like nothing better than for you to simply give up training your tongue to speak life. But even Jesus knew that sometimes a temple has to be cleaned out more than once.

Shortly after Jesus's first miracle at the wedding of Cana, He traveled to Capernaum with His mother, brothers, and disciples. It was almost time for the Jewish Passover celebration, so Jesus went up to Jerusalem to worship. As He approached the temple, Jesus heard the bleating of sheep, smelled the stench of the cattle, and saw the gypsy-like haggling and exchanging of coins. The temple had become a free-for-all rather than a house of prayer.

> So he made a whip out of cords, and drove all from the temple courts, both sheep and cattle; he scattered the coins of the money changers and overturned their tables. To those who sold doves he said, "Get these out of here! Stop turning my Father's house into a market!" (John 2:15-16).

Yes, Jesus cleaned out the temple that day, but it wasn't long before the money changers began to creep back in with their wares. Three years later, during His last week of life on earth, Jesus came upon the unholy mess again.

> Jesus entered the temple courts and drove out all who were buying and selling there. He overturned the tables of the money changers and the benches of those selling doves. "It is written," he said to them, "My house will be called a house of prayer," but you are making it a "den of robbers" (Matthew 21:12-13).

How did the messy mayhem of the temple happen the second time? I don't think it happened all at once. After Jesus cleared out the temple initially, I suspect it stayed that way for a time. But one day, a money changer set up his table. Then another brought in a few birds, followed by a couple of sheep, and then here came a cow.

The next thing you know, the temple wasn't any different than it was before Jesus cleared it out and cleaned it up three years earlier. In three years, it had reverted back to an unholy mess.

And God whispers in my ear: "Do you not know that your bodies are temples of the Holy Spirit, who is in you, whom you have received from God? You are not your own" (1 Corinthians 6:19).

Sometimes I am that messy temple. I bet you are too.

Swept-clean sinful behavior, ungodly thoughts, jump-off-the-cliff emotions, and caustic words are itching to creep back in at all times. It is up to me (and to you) to keep the temple clean.

Perhaps you've had a Holy Spirit moment at some point in your life—a moment that caused you to make a major change in the words you speak. But for the moment to maintain momentum, we need to be constantly aware of our tendency to revert…to go back to the way we were. And remember, you are never on your own. God has given you the power of the Holy Spirit to help you every step of the way.

Psychologists tell us that it takes 21 days to establish a new habit. Here's an idea. For 21 days, put five pennies in your left pocket. Each time you say an encouraging word to someone, move a penny to the right pocket. Make it your goal to move all the pennies from the left to the right and deposit encouraging words to those you come in contact with each day. You'll be doing more than moving pennies. You'll be retraining your mind and establishing new habit patterns for speaking life.

Now that we've looked at the principles for taming the tongue, let's get specific and zero in on a few specific areas with a big impact on those around us.

The Graveyard of Grumbling and the Life Force of Gratitude

Piglet noticed that even though he had a Very Small Heart,
it could hold a rather large amount of Gratitude.

A.A. MILNE

When I was 20 years old, I flew with a team of five to Nevis, West Indies, for a dental mission trip. Like six sardines in an aluminum can, we sat shoulder to shoulder in the rickety twin-engine plane flying low to the ground. The mission was to provide dental care for the poverty-stricken inhabitants of a tiny island with 90 percent unemployment.

With a newly acquired degree in dental hygiene, I was thrilled to join a dentist and his team for a week of ministering to the men, women, and children of this tropical island. We had so much to give to a people who had so little...or so I thought.

The prop plane that taxied us over to the island was too small to take our equipment and luggage in the same trip. Then some men decided we didn't really need our clothes, so they loaded the equipment into the hull, and our clothes were to follow later in the day. Our clothes arrived three days later. Our motto became, "Tell me what you need, and I'll tell you how you can do without it."

What did we encounter on the island? There was poverty. That I expected. There were many dental needs. For that I was prepared. What I did not anticipate was the joy I saw on the faces of the 12 children who lived in a one-room thatched shack with no running water and a packed dirt floor, the contentment of the woman who had one dress and worn-through shoes, the satisfaction of the men who filled their bellies with food from the ocean and tropical fruit that sprang from the surrounding flora. I did not expect the melodic praises to God that rose through the church roofs, the laughter of children dressed in tattered rags, or the coos of mothers contentedly holding their babies to their breasts. I had arrogantly come to help these people, but they had helped me. I experienced what Charles Spurgeon penned: "He is richest who is content with the least." I left wanting to become a woman of gratitude.

THE INFECTION OF EDEN

Do you want to know how to clear a room? How to drive away friends? How to rear sour-faced children? How to make church folks turn their heads when they see you coming? How to stay at a dead-end job? How to get passed over for a promotion? How to get your husband to watch more television? Here's the recipe: complaining, grumbling, murmuring, with a hefty dose of ingratitude thrown in the mix.

For some people—dare I say most?—complaining seems to be a way of life. It's the default mode when we're not intentionally grateful. Constant complaining is draining, frustrating, and annoying to those who have to listen. And if we keep it up, we'll have fewer people who want to listen to us. Period.

A friend of mine and I were looking through his mother's high school yearbook. In the accolades for the seniors, his mom was dubbed "class grumbler." I'm not kidding. And from the time she was 17 to the time she left this earth at 82, she grumbled. Little things, big things. It didn't matter. There was always something to complain about. And she always wondered why she didn't have many friends.

Webster's defines *grumbling* as "to complain in a persistent, bad tempered way; to make a low growling sound."[1] Joshua Rothman notes that the original word also applies to the sound an animal makes: "murmuring, snuffling, growling between your teeth."[2] He goes on: "Grumblers need only a few small dissatisfactions to begin their grumble-some work; from there, one grumble leads naturally to the next. If complaining creates a crisis, grumbling creates an atmosphere."[3]

There's great power in the words of a woman who speaks critical malcontent where nothing is ever good enough, and it's always destructive. Grumbling never makes anything better, and often makes matters worse. Words spoken through the filter of self-centered discontentment are fingernails on the chalkboard of heaven...and we need to stop it.

When did we women start all this complaining, grumbling, and murmuring? Wouldn't you know, it all started with Eve. Most know the story of what happened when the serpent tempted Eve with the forbidden fruit from the tree of the knowledge of good and evil in Genesis 3. But have you ever wondered what made Eve ripe for Satan's picking? I believe it was ingratitude. She had everything a woman could ever want: safety, security, and plenty. She had community with God and harmony with Adam. She had no clothes to wash, no groceries to buy, and no in-laws to contend with. And yet, when the serpent said that God wasn't telling the truth, and she could have more, she believed him. "'You will not certainly die,' the serpent said to the woman. 'For God knows that when you eat from it your eyes will be opened, and you will be like God, knowing good and evil'" (Genesis 3:4-5). Think about it: If Adam and Eve had been grateful for all God had provided for them and the communion they had with Him, they never would have believed the serpent's lie that God was holding out on them.

After they ate the fruit, God confronted them about what they had done.

"The wife *You gave me* made me do it," Adam complained.

"The serpent *You created* made me do it," Eve grumbled.

And the grumbling didn't stop there. From Genesis to Revelation, grumbling rolls through history like a human freight train headed for a cliff. Grumbling is an outward expression of an inward attitude of ingratitude. It squeezes eyes shut to God's goodness and has the power to infect those around us.

Words spoken through the filter of self-centered discontentment are fingernails on the chalkboard of heaven.

THE ROADBLOCK OF GRUMBLING

Ingratitude laced with grumbling, complaining, and murmuring is an easy trap to fall into. And it's highly contagious. Someone grumbles, and the next thing you know, you fall right in line and start grumbling too. I wonder if that's what happened in the wilderness as the Israelites made one more trek around Mount Sinai.

Think of all God had done for the Israelites headed for the Promised Land in the book of Exodus. He'd brought them out of Egyptian slavery, parted the Red Sea for them to walk across on dry land, and called the water to return to its borders to drown the pursuing enemies. After they crossed the ravine, they used their words to praise God! Hallelujahs all around! Miriam even led the worship team. But then they grew thirsty, and "the people *grumbled* against Moses, saying, 'What are we to drink?'" (Exodus 15:24).

God told Moses to throw a piece of wood in the water; it became pure, and they drank. And they were content…for about a minute. A few days later, they grew hungry.

"In the desert the whole community *grumbled* against Moses and Aaron. The Israelites said to them, 'If only we had died by the LORD's hand in Egypt! There we sat around pots of meat and ate all the food we wanted, but you have brought us out into this desert to starve this entire assembly to death'" (Exodus 16:2-3).

They romanticized about the "good old days," which weren't good at all. Another easy trap to fall into. Let's see what happened next.

> So Moses and Aaron said to all the Israelites, "In the evening you will know that it was the LORD who brought you out of Egypt, and in the morning you will see the glory of

the LORD, because he has heard *your grumbling against him.*
Who are we, that you should *grumble* against us?"…Moses
also said, "You will know that it was the LORD when he
gives you meat to eat in the evening and all the bread you
want in the morning, because he has heard your *grumbling*
against him. Who are we? You are not *grumbling* against us,
but against the LORD" (Exodus 16:6-8).

So God rained down manna and quail from heaven. And they were
content…for about a minute. They got thirsty again, and they grumbled. "But the people were thirsty for water there, and they *grumbled*
against Moses. They said, 'Why did you bring us up out of Egypt to
make us and our children and livestock die of thirst'" (Exodus 17:3).

So God brought forth water from a rock, and they were content…
for about a minute. And finally, a few months after leaving Egypt, it
was time for the Israelites to enter the Promised Land. But when they
sent in the spies to check out the fruits of the land, they came back
reporting that very large men lived there. So what did the people do?
They grumbled: "All the Israelites *grumbled* against Moses and Aaron,
and the whole assembly said to them, 'If only we had died in Egypt!
Or in this wilderness! Why is the LORD bringing us to this land only to
die by the sword?'" (Numbers 14:2).

Finally, God said, "Enough." "In this wilderness your bodies will
fall—every one of you twenty years old or more…who has *grumbled*
against me" (Numbers 14:29). The grumblers spent the next 40 years
wandering in the desert. God waited until that entire generation died
out and a new generation rose up who would believe the promises of
God rather than grumble about the problems of man.

How do you think the grumbling and complaining started in the
wilderness? I think it went something like this. A woman came out
of her tent one morning to gather her daily allotment of manna. She
picked up the sweet bread and complained to her neighbor, "You know,
I'm sick of this manna." Then the neighbor looked at the manna in her
basket and said, "You know, I'm sick of it too." Then the next person
agreed. Before they knew it, they were kvetching about everything and

became a sea of ingrates—a tidal wave of grumblers taking one more lap around Mount Sinai while God placed a "Do Not Enter" sign in front of the Promised Land.

Sometimes our grumbling can keep us out of *our* own personal promised land. It certainly did for them. Grumbling and complaining can damage our relationship with others, our fellowship with God, and our ambassadorship for Christ. Grumbling is a roadblock to recognizing and realizing the promises of God.

Grumbling is a roadblock to recognizing and realizing the promises of God.

HOW TO MAKE YOUR PHONE RING LESS

Dr. Guy Winch, in his book *The Squeaky Wheel*, says that we have become a nation of squeakers who complain about everything from bad politicians to bad pedicures with equal vigor. He goes on to say, "Over the decades, complaints devolved from being a goal directed and useful activity to a national pastime. We have become a nation of squeakers who face daily frustrations, resentments, and irritations without a clue as how to address them effectively."[4]

Speaking of pedicures, I wonder if your toes have been hurting reading this chapter as much as mine did writing it. I never thought of myself as a big grumbler until I considered these words of Dr. Winch:

> Most of our complaints are not significant to our mental health in and of themselves. Bacteria are tiny organisms, but taken together, their mass is bigger than all other living things on earth combined. Similarly the vast majority of our complaints are also small. For example: "It's hot." "You're late." "Again, the aisle seat?" "This needs salt." "Now

it's too salty." Their combined volume overshadows our positive utterances combined.[5]

That hurts my toes, and I'm guilty as charged. Those sorts of complaints create an atmosphere in our homes, workplaces, and relationships. We have the power to change that atmosphere, sometimes by simply changing our tone and offering a gentle solution.

For example, grumbling to a server at a restaurant, "This soup is too cold," is a nonproductive complaint and sends a chill around the table. However, saying, "This soup is too cold. Would you mind warming it up for me a bit?" offers a solution and keeps the tone positive. You have the power to adjust the emotional thermostat from chilly to warm by simply tweaking your words and offering a positive solution. Also, thinking of those two discourses spoken to the waiter, which one would you rather have spoken to you?

There is nobody more miserable than an ungrateful person. Margaret and I were chatting about gratitude when she mentioned how she tries to steer clear of those who grumble and complain because their ingratitude is so contagious. "I hate calling my sister," she mused. "I mean, I love her. But talking to her is such a joy drain."

"What do you mean?" I asked.

"All she does is complain. Something is always wrong with her house. She always has a new ailment. She gives me the latest obituary report and tells me who is sick with what. A couple of times I tried to cheer her up. You know, help her see the positive side of things. 'At least you have a house. Think of all those people who lost their homes in the hurricane.' But it only made her mad. She said I was not being sympathetic and that I made little of her problems. So now I just listen."

No one likes to be around a grumbler, and it's a surefire way to make your phone ring less.

THE CURE FOR COMPLAINING

While ingratitude was the infection of Eden, the cure comes in capsules of praise, thanksgiving, and a grateful heart. If complaining, grumbling, and murmuring are fingernails scratching on the chalkboard of heaven, then thanksgiving, praise, and gratitude are the love language of God that enable us to communicate with Him on an intimate level.

Paul wrote to the Thessalonians, "Give thanks in all circumstances" (1 Thessalonians 5:18). Notice the Bible doesn't command us to *feel* thankful in all circumstances. Instead it commands us to "give thanks in all circumstances."

When I begin to praise God in a difficult situation, even if I don't feel like it, my perspective changes. That was a lesson Corrie ten Boom learned from her sister Betsie as they suffered together in a German concentration camp during World War II. They lived in Barracks 28 in overcrowded, filthy conditions and nauseating stench. Reeking straw. Rancid beds. Overflowing toilets. And fleas.

> On their first day in the barracks, as Corrie was fighting the nausea from the reeking straw, and the fleas were biting her one after another, she cried out, "Betsie, how can we live in such a place!" And Betsie remembered a Bible verse they had read that very day. First Thessalonians 5:18: "Give thanks in all circumstances."
>
> "That's it, Corrie!" Betsie exclaimed. "That's His answer. 'Give thanks in all circumstances!' That's what we can do. We can start right now to thank God for every single thing about this new barracks!"
>
> Corrie stared at her sister, then around the dark, foul-aired room and wondered what in the world they had to be thankful for. With Betsie's help, she agreed to give thanks for the fact that they were together, that they snuck a Bible into the camp, and that the overcrowded conditions made it possible for more women to hear the Scriptures when they read each day. But she could not see clear to thank God for the fleas.
>
> "The fleas!" she cried. "This is too much. Betsie. There's no way even God can make me grateful for a flea."

"Give thanks in all circumstances," Betsie quoted. "It doesn't say, 'in pleasant circumstances.' Fleas are part of this place where God has put us."

And so they stood between tiers of bunks and gave thanks for fleas. But this time Corrie was sure Betsie was wrong.

One evening Corrie got back to the barracks late from a wood-gathering foray outside the walls. Betsie was waiting for her, as always, so that they could wait through the food line together. Her eyes were twinkling.

"You're looking extraordinarily pleased with yourself," Corrie told her.

"You know, we've never understood why we had so much freedom in the big room," Betsie replied. "Well—I've found out. This afternoon, there'd been confusion in our knitting group about sock sizes and they'd asked the supervisor to come and settle it. But she wouldn't. She wouldn't step through the door and neither would the guards. And you know why?"

Betsie could not keep the triumph from her voice: "Because of the fleas! That's what she said. That place is crawling with fleas!"[6]

Sometimes I don't see God in difficult situations, but I still can praise Him because I know He is there. Gratitude changes the lens through which we see the circumstances in our little slice of time. Thanksgiving changes our perspective despite shattered dreams, broken relationships, and heartrending circumstances. It changes our perspective in the accumulation of little nuisances in just plain old everyday life. When I find something to be thankful for in a difficult situation or an irritating circumstance, even if I don't feel like it, many times I begin to *feel* thankful. And the amazing thing is, my positive words affect those around me. Sarah Ban Breathnach once said, "Gratitude bestows reverence, allowing us to encounter everyday epiphanies, those transcendent moments of awe that change forever how we experience life (is it abundant or is it lacking?) and the world (is it friendly or is it hostile?)."[7] And how we choose to experience life affects how those around us experience life as well.

Let me share a story that greatly impacted me from my book *Take Hold of the Faith You Long For:*

> One day I was in the airport headed to New Jersey. It was a typical rush, rush, rush morning. Grab the bags, trudge through traffic, hunt for a parking space, follow the herd, wade through security, dash to the gate.
>
> Folks aren't usually very friendly in airports. Eyes look straight ahead. Purposed feet slap the floor. Overstuffed bags roll behind. It's not that people are grumpy. They're just "flatish." (That's a new word for today.)
>
> On this particular morning, I looked just like everyone else. "Flatish."
>
> Before settling in at my gate, I decided to make one last trip to the restroom. I'm so glad I did. It was one of the most joy-filled places I had been in a long time.
>
> Gretchen, the "hostess" for this privy, donned a silly little hat on her head with whimsical feathers waving about the top. If it wasn't for the official attendant's vest she was wearing, I might have thought she was on her way to Mardi Gras. With a spray bottle in one hand and a cloth in the other, Gretchen welcomed each "guest" into her "home."
>
> "Come right this way," she cheered as she opened a stall door for her next visitor.
>
> A woman in a green jacket exited a stall, and Gretchen swooped in behind her. Squirt, squirt, squirt with the disinfectant. Wipe, wipe, wipe with her cloth.
>
> "Right this way, madam," she motioned to the next person in line, "This one is ready for you! Come right in!"
>
> With all the poise of a valet opening the castle doors for

a person of honor, Gretchen welcomed each woman as if she were the most important person in her day. I stood back and watched as this five-foot five-inch bundle of joy wiped off toilet seats and cheerfully invited her next guest into the pristine stalls. Gretchen had an effervescent sense of joy…wiping toilet seats. It seemed to come from a deep-seated heart of gratitude. And it spilled over to every single woman who left her station.

Women entered weary and worn and left with a skip in their step and a smile on their face. Some even lingered… as if they wanted to soak in just a little bit more before facing the world. I was one of them.

On the counter rested a tip jar filled to the brim with thanks. But I don't think the "tips" were for wiping the germs away from the toilet seats, but for wiping the doldrums away from their hearts and frowns off of their faces. And for some strange reason, I just wanted to give Gretchen a hug. I did. She didn't mind.

Gretchen reminded me just how contagious gratitude and joy can be, and how desperately I want to be a carrier.[8]

Did you see it? I wonder what my attitude would have been cleaning toilets in a public facility. I know what my attitude is when I clean toilets in my own home! Are my spoken words affecting those around me? Are my words swimming about in my head affecting my own personal joy?

When we live a life of intentional gratitude and speak words of thanksgiving, we begin to frame how we see our circumstances. Then how we speak about those circumstances affects how others around us see them as well. A child mirrors his mom's response to a certain situation. A friend begins to see the upside of a difficult situation. A husband sees the possibilities in a seemingly impossible situation.

In Henry Ward Beecher's words: "Pride slays thanksgiving…a proud man is seldom a grateful man, for he never thinks he gets as much as he deserves."[9] I am reminded of an old saying that stirs and stings: "Gratitude turns what we have into enough." Always enough. Jesus thanked God for the two loaves and five fish…and there was more than enough to go around (John 6:1-13).

Paul wrote, "Rejoice in the Lord always. I will say it again (because you probably didn't get it the first time): Rejoice!" (Philippians 4:4, parentheses mine). "Rejoice in the Lord" doesn't mean only when we're in church. It includes life as we live and move and have our being in Him (Acts 17:28).

If complaining, grumbling, and murmuring are fingernails scratching on the chalkboard of heaven, then thanksgiving, praise, and gratitude are the love language of God that enable us to communicate with Him on an intimate level.

THE MEMORY OF THE HEART

I put my favorite photos in frames so I can see them often. They bring me joy as I pass through a room. A smiling five-year-old Steven with his brand-new golden retriever puppy. A strong man-child dressed in a graduation cap and gown. A passel of sun-kissed nieces and nephews standing on the beach with laughing faces. My husband and son wading in the lake at sunset ready to be baptized together. These are pictures that say…*remember.*

The problem with the grumbling Israelites is that they experienced spiritual amnesia. Time and time again they forgot about God's protection and provision. And there's a cure for that as well! *Remembering.*

Gratitude has been called the "memory of the heart."[10] Praise and gratitude bring up pictures in our minds that say, "Remember." Remember what God has done and is doing in your life. Journal about it. Tell about it. Make a list of all you have to be thankful for and add to it often.

Remember how God protected you from making a terrible decision.

Remember how God brought you to your spouse.

Remember how God healed you or your loved one from that disease.

Remember how God saved you from that terrible accident.

Remember the impossible situation from which God delivered you.

Remember how God didn't give you what you wanted, but exactly what you needed.

Remember the unexpected rainbow.

Remember the phone call that came at just the right time.

WHO ARE WE COMPLAINING AGAINST?

Complaining is a casual despising of God's sovereignty. It's like saying we don't like how He is running things and think we could do it better. Grumbling isn't really about our circumstances, but about how we feel God is handling our circumstances. Oh sure, it might sound like we're complaining that the service is slow, the weather is horrible, the kids are inconsiderate, the husband is inattentive, the praise music is too loud. (I'm sorry. How can praise be too loud? Isn't that better than being too quiet? I digress.) But, ultimately, it's not about the service, the weather, the kids, the husband, or the music. We're complaining about how God's running the universe.

Isn't that what Moses said to the Israelites? "In the morning you will see the glory of the LORD, because he has heard *your grumbling against him*. Who are we, that you should *grumble* against us?" (Exodus 16:7).

Job was a man who lost everything, yet he didn't complain. His wife, on the other hand, suggested he curse God and die (Job 2:9). But Job's reply was, "You are talking like a foolish woman. Shall we accept good from God, and not trouble?" His contentment did not rely on people, position, or possessions, but on the knowledge of the sovereignty of God.

In the New Testament, we see a mirrored example in the person of Paul. Paul had been a man of influence who graduated from the best schools with a degree of a Pharisee and had been born into the elite line of Benjamin. He referred to himself as a faultless Hebrew of Hebrews with legalistic righteousness. But *after* he came to Christ, not before, his life was riddled with persecution, problems, and prison. Yet he wrote, "*I have learned* the secret of being content in any and every situation, whether well fed or hungry, whether living in plenty or in want. I can do all this through him who gives me strength" (Philippians 4:11-13).

Where was Paul when he penned these words? He was under house arrest, chained to a Roman guard 24 hours a day. Paul knew that living in union with Christ was the true source of contentment. Amazingly, in this letter to the Philippians, his key message is "Rejoice!"

I'm struck by the phrase he used twice in these verses and once in another: "I have learned" (4:11)…"I have learned" (4:12)…"Put it into practice" (4:9). And there's the secret for living a life of gratitude that silences the grumbling. *I have learned…Put it into practice.* The Greek word used for *learned* here means not only to know factually but also to obey practically.[11] Perhaps speaking words of gratitude and thanksgiving doesn't come naturally, but it will come supernaturally with practice.[12] And yet, gratitude only comes to those who open their eyes to the goodness of God rather than negatively nitpicking and putting discontentment on display. Paul shows us how to speak words of gratitude whether empty or full, whether walking on the beach or chained to a Roman guard.

During Paul's arrest, he was not only captive, but he also had a captive audience. He was able to have one-on-one time with the guards. Not only was he able to share the gospel with them, but they were privy to the conversations between Paul and his many visitors. Paul's time in prison also gave him time to write letters to the churches, which we hold in our hands today in the New Testament. What we might see as a problem to grumble about, God wants to use as a provision for which we can be grateful.

Paul's words, "I can do all things through Him who strengthens me" (Philippians 4:13 NASB), was one of the first Bible verses I learned as a new Christian. I applied it to every hurdle imaginable. But the truth is, Paul wrote this verse in the context of contentment in the ups and downs of life. I can only imagine how Paul's words of gratitude, thanksgiving, and contentment affected those Roman guards every day. I suspect it was the same way *our* words of gratitude, thanksgiving, and contentment affect those around us every day.

Gratitude only comes to those who open their eyes to the goodness of God rather than negatively nitpicking and putting discontentment on display.

PRACTICAL STEPS TO GROWING GRATITUDE

So what do you do if you've looked in the mirror and seen a grumbler looking back at you? First, let me note that psychologists say that not all complaining is bad. For example, complaining about social injustice shows that you are concerned and empathetic. But productive complaining—the best sort—provides a possible solution in the process.

Let's take some practical steps for complaint restraint protocol. I'm doing it with you.

1. Pray and ask God to make you aware of your grumbling and complaining. Pray that God will set a guard over your mouth and keep watch over the door of your lips (Psalm 141:3).

2. Catch yourself before the words come out of your mouth.

3. When you feel the urge to complain, try to think of a positive solution before you speak.

4. Realize that we live in a culture of complaining, and make a decision to not conform to the pattern of this world (Romans 12:2).

5. If you find yourself complaining about work or a relationship, stop grumbling and address the issue in a productive way. For example, if you complain about work to your family, and family to your work, stop it. Address the work issue at work and the family issue at home.

6. Avoid complaining as a conversation starter. For example, "I'm so tired of this rain" starts the conversation on a negative path.

7. If someone around you complains, resist the urge to join in. Affirm the person by acknowledging his or her comment with something like, "I hear you!" But, then lead the conversation in a more positive direction.

8. Don't complain about someone else's complaining or ignore their complaint. Most likely your complaint about their complaining will fuel their frustration, make them feel judged, and create distance in the relationship. You can say, "I'm sorry you feel that way," or "I'm sorry that happened to you" to show you're listening. But don't join in grumblings with your own.

9. Be flexible and resist expecting situations, circumstances, or people to be a certain way.

10. Realize that inconveniences may be divine appointments. Establish a no complaining zone for 21 days. If you catch yourself in a complaint, then write down three reasons to be thankful.

THE SMILEY FACE ON THE WINDOW

I was flying home from Pennsylvania on Good Friday of the Easter weekend, and the airport was packed. As I waited for the plane to arrive at the gate, clouds began to fill the sky. Unfortunately, overbooked airplanes and stormy weather do not a good combination make. Delays and cancellations lit up the departure board.

I was scheduled to arrive in Charlotte at 7:00 p.m. But then my arrival time was pushed back to 7:40, then to 8:40, then to 9:00. This was turning out to be not such a "good Friday" after all. The travelers were getting angry, the ticketing agents were getting agitated, and kids were getting antsy. I just wanted to go home.

Finally, after many gate changes and time delays, we boarded the plane headed for Charlotte. I closed my eyes and went to sleep. About an hour later, the pilot made an announcement.

"Hello, this is the captain. Unfortunately, the storm is passing through Charlotte, NC, at this time, and we will not be able to land. We are going to land in Greensboro, 90 miles away, and wait it out. Feel free to disembark the airplane, but do not leave the boarding area. We will make an announcement when it is time to reboard. Don't worry, we'll get you to Charlotte just as quickly as possible. Sorry for the inconvenience."

We landed in Greensboro and waited…and waited…and waited. About 10:30, there was another announcement. "May I have your attention please? For those traveling on flight 389 to Charlotte, unfortunately, the flight crew has logged in too many hours, and they will not be able to continue the flight to Charlotte. We have secured vans to drive you the rest of the way. Sorry for the inconvenience."

You could just hear the collective moan. We trudged down to baggage claim, retrieved our bags, and separated into groups of nine.

And we waited.

A man in a business suit, trying to pass the time with polite banter, asked me, "So, what do you do?"

I cut my eyes over at him and said, "I'd rather not say." Thinking he might get the wrong idea, I smiled and said, "Just kidding. I'm an author."

"What do you write?"

I was hoping he wouldn't ask me that. I took a deep breath and said, "I write Christian oriented books for women that help them learn how to handle the difficulties of life." We all started laughing.

We piled into the van: eight traveling to visit family, one going home. We quickly learned that the air conditioner was broken, and rather than cool air coming through the vents, heat poured out in every direction. No one could figure out how to shut it off. Temperatures rose, sweat poured, layers came off, the windows fogged up. It was miserable.

After about an hour and a half, I started to relax, thinking we would be in Charlotte at any minute. In the seat in front of me, a twentysomething woman and her mother chatted happily. They were on their way to spend the weekend with daughter number two. Daughter number one, who was apparently tracking our progress on her smartphone, turned around in her seat to face me.

"We're passing Statesville," she said. "How much further do we have?"

"Statesville!" I cried. "We're not supposed to be passing Statesville! He's going the wrong way!"

Our one-and-a-half-hour van ride turned into a three-hour trip. I was ready for this not-so-good Friday to be over. And it just about was because it was close to midnight.

Just as I was having a not-so-nice, one-way conversation with God, the mother in front of me drew a smiley face on the steamed-up window! A smiley face!

What in the world does she have to be happy about! I mused. *I don't see anything "smiley" about this entire situation!*

We finally arrived in Charlotte sometime after midnight. The quick one-and-a-half-hour flight had turned into an eight-hour nightmare. Nine dripping-wet, exhausted passengers climbed out of the van and breathed in the fresh night air.

"Bye, Krista," I said to the young, smartphone-toting girl. "You have fun with your sister and mom this weekend."

"Oh, we will," she said. "My mom just found out that she has cancer for the second time. It doesn't look too good. We're going to spend a weekend together, just the three of us, simply enjoying each other. It might be our last."

She turned to walk away...never seeing the tears that filled my eyes.

I looked back at the van's window, which still held the picture of a smiley face drawn by a dying woman's hand. Suddenly, my night of little inconveniences seemed rather petty.

It was a Good Friday after all. God had reminded me of all the reasons I had to be thankful. Irritating circumstances are a sure thing in this world. Storms will rage. Winds of adversity will blow. It is our perspective in the storm that will determine whether we will grumble and complain or draw a smiley face on the window and thank God for each and every breath we have. There is always a choice.

I slipped into the car with my precious, patient husband, gave him a quick kiss, and drew a smiley face on the window.

When we look at the difficulties, inconveniences, and problems of life as potential assignments from God, our perspectives change. We can decide to focus on what God can do through a difficult circumstance rather than the details of the circumstance itself.

We can't control our circumstances, but we do have a choice as to how we react to them. Chuck Swindoll reminds us:

> Words can never adequately convey the incredible impact of our attitude toward life. The longer I live the more convinced I become that life is 10 percent what happens to you and 90 percent how we respond to it...I believe the single most important decision I can make on a day-to-day basis is my choice of attitude. It is more important than my past, my education, my bankroll, my successes or failures, fame or pain, what other people think of me or say about me, my circumstances, or my position. Attitude is that "single string" that keeps me going or cripples my progress. It alone fuels my fire or assaults my hope. When my attitudes are right, there's no barrier too high, no valley too deep, no dream too extreme, no challenge too great for me.[13]

Bible Verses About Complaining

1. Moses also said, "You will know that it was the Lord when he gives you meat to eat in the evening and all the bread you want in the morning, because he has heard your grumbling against him. Who are we? You are not grumbling against us, but against the Lord" (Exodus 16:8).

2. How long will this wicked community grumble against me? I have heard the complaints of these grumbling Israelites (Numbers 14:27).

3. In this wilderness your bodies will fall—every one of you twenty years old or more who was counted in the census and who has grumbled against me (Numbers 14:29).

4. A quarrelsome wife is like the dripping of a leaky roof in a rainstorm (Proverbs 27:15).

5. It's better to live alone in the desert than with a quarrelsome, *complaining* wife (Proverbs 21:19 NLT).

6. "Stop grumbling among yourselves," Jesus answered (John 6:43).

7. Do everything without grumbling or arguing (Philippians 2:14).

8. Offer hospitality to one another without grumbling (1 Peter 4:9).

9. Don't grumble against one another, brothers and sisters, or you will be judged (James 5:9).

10. Enoch, who lived in the seventh generation after Adam, prophesied about these people. He said, "Listen! The Lord is coming with countless thousands of his holy ones to execute judgment on the people of the world. He will convict every person of all the ungodly things they have

done and for all the insults that ungodly sinners have spoken against him." These people are grumblers and complainers, living only to satisfy their desires. They brag loudly about themselves, and they flatter others to get what they want (Jude 14-16 NLT).

Bible Verses About Gratitude

1. Shout for joy to the LORD, all the earth.
   Worship the LORD with gladness;
     come before him with joyful songs.
   Know that the LORD is God.
   It is he who made us, and we are his;
     we are his people, the sheep of his pasture.
   Enter his gates with thanksgiving
     and his courts with praise;
     give thanks to him and praise his name.
   For the LORD is good and his love endures forever;
     his faithfulness continues through all generations
     (Psalm 100:1-5).

2. Give thanks to the LORD, for he is good;
     his love endures forever (Psalm 107:1).

3. You are my God, and I will praise you;
     you are my God, and I will exalt you.
   Give thanks to the LORD, for he is good;
     his love endures forever (Psalm 118:28-29).

4. Rejoice always, pray continually, give thanks in all circumstances; for this is God's will for you in Christ Jesus (1 Thessalonians 5:16-18).

5. Do not get drunk on wine, which leads to debauchery. Instead, be filled with the Spirit, speaking to one another with psalms, hymns, and songs from the Spirit. Sing and make music from your heart to the Lord, always giving

thanks to God the Father for everything, in the name of our Lord Jesus Christ (Ephesians 5:18-20).

6. Do not be anxious about anything, but in every situation, by prayer and petition, with thanksgiving, present your requests to God. And the peace of God, which transcends all understanding, will guard your hearts and your minds in Christ Jesus (Philippians 4:6-7).

7. So then, just as you received Christ Jesus as Lord, continue to live your lives in him, rooted and built up in him, strengthened in the faith as you were taught, and overflowing with thankfulness (Colossians 2:6-7).

8. Let the peace of Christ rule in your hearts, since as members of one body you were called to peace. And be thankful (Colossians 3:15).

9. And whatever you do, whether in word or deed, do it all in the name of the Lord Jesus, giving thanks to God the Father through him (Colossians 3:17).

10. Devote yourselves to prayer, being watchful and thankful (Colossians 4:2).

"Gratitude...turns what we have into enough, and more. It turns denial into acceptance, chaos into order, confusion into clarity...Gratitude makes sense of our past, brings peace for today, and creates a vision for tomorrow" —Melody Beattie.[14]

12

The Melody of Silence

A closed mouth gathers no foot.

Author Unknown

From the time I could hold a crayon in my chubby little hand, I've enjoyed creating various "works of art." Many of those masterpieces ended up under the Christmas trees for family and friends. One year, it was macramé hanging plant holders. Another, it was a menagerie of decoupage wooden boxes. Then there were the years of framed cross-stitch, ceramic nativity sets, and quilted pig and chicken pillows (don't laugh).

When I was 17, it was the year of the candle. Everyone from Grandma Edwards to my best friends received praying hand candles. For weeks I slaved over a hot stove, stirring melted wax, meticulously centering ten-inch wicks, then slowly pouring the red, green, or yellow molten material into inverted molds in the shape of praying hands. When the wax hardened, I burped the rubber mold and plopped out the candle. My kitchen looked like a prosthesis laboratory with hands littering the counters.

One night I was cooking up a fresh batch of hands when the doorbell rang. "Oh, my word!" I cried as I glanced at the clock on the oven. "Jim's here!"

I was having so much fun waxing and wicking that I forgot the time.

I had a date at 7:30, and here I was in pink hot curlers and a paraffin-covered sweatshirt. I rushed through the kitchen, leaped over my dad who had fallen asleep on the den floor in front of the television, and threw open the door.

"Hi, Jim," I huffed. "Come on in. I'm sorry. I'm not ready."

"So I noticed," he said with a grin.

"I was cooking candles and lost track of time."

"You were what?"

"Never mind. Just come on in and have a seat on the couch. I'll be ready in a minute."

I dashed to my room to run a brush through my hair, swipe mascara through my lashes, and place a hint of gloss on my lips. Jim sat uncomfortably on the sofa, listening to my father snore to the bantering of Jackie Gleason and Ralph Kramden. After about 15 minutes, Jim smelled something burning. He didn't want to yell for me for fear of waking up my dad, so he tiptoed into the kitchen and discovered a pot sitting on the stove with flames shooting up about 18 inches in the air.

Sleeping dad or no sleeping dad, Jim called out. "Sharon! Whatever you were cooking is on fire!"

"Oh, my goodness!" I exclaimed. "I forgot to turn the stove off!"

Just as I burst into the kitchen, Jim threw a cup of water into the flaming wax. Rather than extinguish the flames, the fire exploded upward. The flames shot up the wall, across the ceiling, and down the wall on the opposite side of the room. Our screams woke my father to see his daughter standing in a room surrounded by flames. With the agility of Superman, Dad sprang to his feet and ran to the kitchen faster than a speeding bullet. He grabbed the lid of the pot and clamped it down on the source of the flames. Just as quickly as the fire had erupted, it receded back into the pot like a genie returning to his bottle.

This all happened in a matter of seconds. We stood in the middle of the room like three stunned deer. I never did tell my dad that it was Jim who threw the water on the burning wax. Teenage boys already have two strikes against them when they walk through the threshold to pick up a man's baby girl.

After the shock wore off, I had time to reflect on the incident:

the speed at which the flames blazed around the room, the feeling of fire licking against my skin, the terrifying sound of the flames. I also learned just how easy it was to stop the blaze. Simply put a lid on it.

Isn't that the way with our words? We can quickly explode with fiery words, and the destruction spreads up one wall and down the other before we even know it. But as soon as my father placed a lid on the pot and removed the flames' source of oxygen, the fire went out. I love what Job said after God put him in his place for questioning His actions: "I put my hand over my mouth" (Job 40:4). It is interesting to me that my hand fits perfectly over my mouth. Go ahead and give it a try. I bet yours does too. Some of us may need two hands, but that's okay! Perhaps that was God's intentional design!

In the last chapter, we looked at how to tame the tongue and move from grumbling to gratitude, but sometimes we simply need to hold the tongue. Oftentimes, the most powerful words of a woman are the ones she will never speak.

LOOSE LIPS SINK RELATION-SHIPS

I love reading WWII books and watching WWII movies and documentaries. During the war, the War Advertising Council created propaganda posters as a part of a campaign to advise servicemen and citizens to avoid careless talk concerning secure information that might be of use by the enemy. The gist of the slogan was to remind people to avoid talking about ship movements. The fear was that covert enemy agents might hear the comments, intercept the war effort, and destroy the ships. Thus, "Loose Lips Sink Ships" signs were posted on factory walls across America.

Loose lips still sink ships. Perhaps we need to hang a sign in our homes that says, "Loose lips sink relation-ships." Choose wisely. Don't allow the loose lips of sarcasm, criticism, or anger to poke holes in the hull of your hunky man or mask of your marvelous kids. A moment of restraint can save a boatload of hurt.

Solomon wrote: "When there are many words, transgression is unavoidable, but he who restrains his lips is wise" (Proverbs 10:19 NASB).

"Even fools are thought wise if they keep silent, and discerning if they hold their tongues" (Proverbs 17:28). Whether the subject is gossip or grumbling, silence is the golden key that keeps the door to destructive words locked away. And sometimes the most powerful words of a woman are no words at all, for silence can be an outward sign of inward strength.

I was having lunch with a group of friends when one made a derogatory comment about one of the group who was late. I gave her that "motherly look" that let her know the comment wasn't appropriate.

"Well, it's true," she said.

"Just because something is true doesn't mean that you should say it," I answered.

You know where I learned that? The Holy Spirit speaks that to me almost every day. Unfortunately, I have ignored Him more times than I'd like to admit, and I have spoken words I have later regretted. Like David, I plead with God to "set a guard over my mouth, Lord; keep watch over the door of my lips" (Psalm 141:3).

The summer before my senior year in high school, I went to France to study language and art with 50 or so students from around the United States. As part of our training, we were allowed to only speak French during mealtimes. If we slipped and said a word in English, we had to put a coin into a bowl in the middle of the table. It was the quietest bunch of teenagers sitting around a dinner table you've ever seen! In reality, saying an inappropriate word will cost more than a few coins. It can cost a relationship. Sometimes the most powerful words are no words at all.

For most of us, it takes years to learn this lesson, but not always. A little girl lost a playmate in death, and one day reported to her family that she had gone to comfort the sorrowing mother. "What did you say?" asked her father. "Nothing," she replied. "I just climbed up on her lap and cried with her." That was exactly what that mother needed.

DID YOU HEAR ABOUT...?

A monster was sneaking into my yard in the dark of night and devouring my prize plants. I never saw his beady eyes or heard his pounding footsteps—just the aftermath of his destruction. He left a trail of slime as he moved from plant to plant, leaving large, gaping holes in broadleaf gerbera daisies; gnawing entire velvety, trumpet-shaped blossoms on purple petunias; and reducing bushy begonias to naked stalks.

I asked a neighbor about my flowerbed's demise, and she said, "You've got slugs."

"Slugs!" I exclaimed. "The yard monster is a tiny little slug?"

"You can put out slug bait to catch them and see for yourself," my confident neighbor continued.

I sprinkled slug bait all around the yard and then waited. The next morning I viewed the "monsters'" remains. The beasts were about a quarter-inch long—about the size of my little toe nail.

How could something so small cause so much damage in such a short amount of time? I mused. Then my mind thought of something else very small that can cause enormous damage in a short amount of time…gossip. King Solomon wrote, "The words of a gossip are like choice morsels; they go down to the inmost parts" (Proverbs 18:8). Just as one tiny slug can destroy an entire flower bed, so can one tiny morsel of gossip destroy a person's reputation, mar one's character, and devour a friendship.

In the South we have this knack for making gossip sound…almost nice. All you have to do is add "bless her heart" to the end of the sentence. It goes like this: "Susie gained 50 pounds with that last pregnancy, bless her heart." "Keesha's husband ran off with his secretary, bless her heart." "I heard Mariah yelling at the postman yesterday, bless her heart." But all the "bless her hearts" don't mask what is really going on…gossip.

Solomon wrote, "Whoever repeats the matter separates close friends" (Proverbs 17:9). Charles Allen, author of *God's Psychiatry,* observed: "Those of great minds discuss ideas, people of mediocre minds discuss events, and those of small minds discuss other people."[1] Maybe if we are spending our time talking about people, we need to fill our minds with better information, such as good books and helpful articles (and I don't mean *People* magazine or the *National Enquirer*).

What exactly is gossip? My dictionary defines *gossip* as "easy, fluent, trivial talk, talk about people behind their backs." It's repeating information about another person's private affairs. If you have to look around to make sure that no one can hear what you are saying, you are probably gossiping. If you would not say something in front of the person you are talking about, then you're probably gossiping.

We have often heard the phrase "knowledge is power." Perhaps that is why gossip is so appealing. It suggests a certain amount of power because "I have the inside scoop." But gossip is not power. On the contrary, it shows a lack of power...a lack of self-control.

But it takes two to tango the gossip dance. "Without wood a fire goes out; without a gossip a quarrel dies down" (Proverbs 26:20). The Bible tells us to make every effort to avoid gossipers (Proverbs 20:19). A good rule of thumb is if you are not part of the problem or part of the solution, then keep the information to yourself.

Paul warned, "Some of you are living idle lives, refusing to work and meddling in other people's business" (2 Thessalonians 3:11 NLT). Other translations call such people "busybodies" (NASB, NIV).

One day a woman felt overwhelmed with guilt over her years of malicious gossip. She went to the local priest and confessed her sin. The priest was all too aware of her wagging tongue and had experienced the sting of her words firsthand...or rather secondhand.

"What can I do to rectify all the damage I have caused with my gossip?" she asked.

"Gather a bag of feathers," he began. "Then go around to each house and place a feather at their door."

That seemed like a simple enough request, so the woman did just as the priest had instructed. After the task was complete, she returned. "I have done what you requested," she said. "Now what am I to do?"

"Now go back and retrieve each of the feathers," he replied.

"That is impossible," the woman argued. "The wind will have blown them all around town by now."

"Exactly," replied the wise priest. "Once you have spoken an ill word, it drifts through the air on wings of gossip, never to be retrieved. God has forgiven you, as you have asked. But I cannot remove the consequences of your hurtful words or gather them from the places they have landed."

Here's an idea. If a friend approaches you with some "news" or a "concern" about another person, stop and ask, "May I quote you on what you're about to tell me?" That will usually put a lid on the conversation before it even begins.

BITING YOUR TONGUE
BUILDS RELATIONSHIPS

Holding our tongue is a discipline worth mastering; however, sometimes we need to *bite* our tongue. Words spoken in anger are daggers to the heart of the listener. I've felt the sharp arrow of angry words pierce my heart, and I've also been the archer with the bow. I know many who have regretted words spoken in anger, but I've never known anyone who regretted withholding them. Sometimes we might actually have to bite down on our tongues to keep them from lashing out when we're mad. Author Karen Ehman wrote, "Better a bleeding tongue than a family member's wounded heart."[2] A great question to ask ourselves before we speak in the heat of the moment is, "What is my hoped-for outcome from the words I'm about to say?"

If it's retaliation, bite down hard.

If it's to shame, bite down hard.

If it's to put the person in his/her place, bite down hard.

If it's to intimidate, bite down hard.

Paul wrote, "In your anger do not sin: Do not let the sun go down while you are still angry, and do not give the devil a foothold" (Ephesians 4:26-27). Paul did not say, "Don't get angry." God created us with a stew of emotions, and anger is one of the ingredients. Even Jesus got angry (Mark 3:5). Paul did say don't let your anger cause you to sin.

So what does it mean to be angry but not sin because of it? There is a righteous kind of anger that is anger at the things that anger God, such as child abuse, sex trafficking, defaming the Holy Spirit. Anger rooted in our sin nature is another matter. That produces "discord, jealousy, fits of rage, selfish ambition, slander, gossip, arrogance, and disorder" (2 Corinthians 12:20). It produces "hatred, discord…fits of rage [i.e. tantrums], selfish ambition, dissensions, [and] factions" (Galatians 5:20). Sinful anger is so common in us that we must be regularly reminded to put away "anger, wrath, [and] malice" (Colossians 3:8 NASB) and that "anyone who is angry with a brother or sister will be subject to judgment" (Matthew 5:22).

The challenge is learning how to manage anger and express it in a productive way. Anger laced with revenge is never productive. Payback is God's department. God said, "It is mine to avenge; I will repay" (Deuteronomy 32:35). When we're angry, stuffing it down is not the answer. Dealing with the anger in a productive way is. When you feel the burning urge to wound with words in anger, take a deep breath.

- Admit that you're angry.
- Count to ten or a hundred.
- Go for a walk.
- Leave the situation to add space to process.
- Ask yourself what about the situation made you so angry. Are you filtering present words through past experience?
- Calm down before you speak.

Remember "A soft answer turns away wrath, but a harsh word stirs up anger" (Proverbs 15:1 ESV). A soft answer doesn't mean that I don't give a truthful answer, but one that is grace-laced. That is so hard to do in the heat of the moment. But I have seen time and time again that when I'm hit with an angry comment, and then let it hang in the air for a bit, the harshness often slaps the one who said it back in the face. However, if I have given an angry comeback, which is what I really want to do, the argument escalates and poof…you've got a formula for sin.

I'm not suggesting we become stuffers who never address issues that stir up anger. I am suggesting that we calm down first, think about what we need to say, and discuss the issue in a productive manner. I know…that's not easy. I've done a lot of walking.

YOU'VE GOT TO KNOW
WHEN TO HOLD 'EM

Back in the day, country singer Kenny Rogers wrote a song that said, "You got to know when to hold 'em / know when to fold 'em." Of course, he was talking about playing cards, but I think the same can be said for playing our words. We've got to know when to hold 'em and know when to fold 'em.

Solomon said it this way: "There is a time for everything, and a season for every activity under the heavens...a time to be silent and a time to speak" (Ecclesiastes 3:1,7). Sometimes the most powerful words are the ones we do not speak. There is a time to speak and a time to keep quiet. The wise woman discerns the difference.

Silence is not always golden. We can use our silence as a weapon to control, punish, or manipulate someone. Many marriages have been wounded by passive-aggressive behavior just as they have been damaged by verbal abuse. When we give someone the cold shoulder or silent treatment for long periods of time, our silence spews our feelings just like an angry outburst. Yes, words can be used as weapons, and silence can be part of the arsenal. So when you're "holding 'em," make sure you're doing it for the right reasons.

Proverbs 31 is one of my favorite chapters in the Bible. Verses 10-31 have served as a plumb line for women throughout the centuries. The verses were actually penned by King Lemuel's mother, instructing him about what to look for in a godly wife. The Proverbs 31 woman wasn't an actual person, but an ideal this wise mother set before her precious son. While the ideal can be quite intimidating to some, all would agree she is a role model worth emulating. Let's think for just a moment about the qualities of this treasured lady. Scripture describes her as smart, crafty, thrifty, and strong. She's a good cook, a savvy money manager, a helper in the community, an entrepreneur, a seamstress, a blessed mother, a faithful friend, a loyal wife, and a lover of God. Whew! That's a lot to take in. Verse 10 begins, "An excellent wife, who can find? For her worth is far above jewels" (NASB). The NIV calls her "a wife of noble character." I like the Amplified version, which says, "a capable, intelligent, and virtuous woman." The Hebrew word that's translated *excellent* or *virtuous* can also mean "wealthy, prosperous, valiant, boldly courageous, powerful, mighty warrior." That sounds strikingly like the *ezer* we met in chapter 5.

In order to help Lemuel remember these character traits, she taught them in the form of an acrostic using the letters of the Hebrew alphabet from beginning to end. The queen knew that among the most important qualities to look for in a wife were the words she spoke. She instructed her son at her knee. "She speaks with wisdom, and faithful instruction is on her tongue" (Proverbs 31:26).

Where does wisdom come from? Does it naturally come with gray hair as old wives' tales have said? Is it obtained through education? Is it a product of intelligence? King Solomon believed wisdom came from God. He sums it up this way: "The fear of the LORD is the beginning of wisdom, and knowledge of the Holy One is understanding" (Proverbs 9:10). Bottom line...wisdom comes from a reverence, knowledge, and understanding of God.

But how does one define wisdom? The *New Open Bible* defines *wisdom* as "knowledge guided by understanding." It can also be defined as the "power of judging rightly and following the soundest course of action, based on knowledge, experience, understanding."

Consider the following verses about wisdom:

> The LORD gives wisdom; from his mouth come knowledge and understanding (Proverbs 2:6).

> Wisdom will save you from the ways of wicked men, from men whose words are perverse (Proverbs 2:12).

> Blessed are those who find wisdom, those who gain understanding, for she is more profitable than silver and yields better returns than gold. She is more precious than rubies; nothing you desire can compare with her (Proverbs 3:13-15).

> Do not forsake wisdom, and she will protect you; love her, and she will watch over you (Proverbs 4:6).

Choose my instruction instead of silver, knowledge rather than choice gold, for wisdom is more precious than rubies, and nothing you desire can compare with her (Proverbs 8:10-11).

The mouth of the righteous flows with wisdom, but the perverted tongue will be cut out (Proverbs 10:31 NASB).

When pride comes, then comes disgrace, but with humility comes wisdom (Proverbs 11:2).

Where there is strife, there is pride, but wisdom is found in those who take advice (Proverbs 13:10).

How much better to get wisdom than gold, to get insight rather than silver! (Proverbs 16:16).

A discerning person keeps wisdom in view, but a fool's eyes wander to the ends of the earth (Proverbs 17:24).

So how do we obtain godly wisdom? It all begins with a personal relationship with Jesus Christ. Paul wrote, "In him [Jesus Christ], we have redemption through his blood, the forgiveness of sins, in accordance with the riches of God's grace that he lavished on us. With all wisdom and understanding" (Ephesians 1:7-8). While our journey to wisdom begins with our belief in Jesus Christ, it continues to grow as our relationship deepens into true intimacy with Him. Paul prayed for the Ephesians, "I keep asking that the God of our Lord Jesus Christ, the glorious Father, may give you the Spirit of wisdom and revelation, so that you may know him better" (Ephesians 1:17).

God is the One who gives us wisdom, but we play a role in the impartation as well. He speaks to us through the pages of the Bible, through prayer, and through the power of the Holy Spirit.

The Bible. "All Scripture is God-breathed and is useful for teaching, rebuking, correcting and training in righteousness, so that the servant of God may be thoroughly equipped for every good work" (2 Timothy 3:16-17).

Prayer. "If any of you lacks wisdom, you should ask God, who gives generously to all without finding fault, and it will be given to you" (James 1:5).

Holy Spirit. "The Spirit searches all things, even the deep things of God. For who knows a person's thoughts except their own spirit within them? In the same way no one knows the thoughts of God except the Spirit of God. What we have received is not the spirit of the world, but the Spirit who is from God, so that we may understand what God has freely given us. This is what we speak, not in words taught us by human wisdom but in words taught by the Spirit, explaining spiritual realities with Spirit-taught words" (1 Corinthians 2:10-13).

God also pours wisdom into our lives through wise people. Solomon warned, "He who walks with wise men will be wise, but the companion of fools will suffer harm" (Proverbs 13:20 NASB). That is why it is so important to have friends who speak wisdom and not foolishness. Their words will be absorbed into your spirit, and the next thing you know...out pops foolishness from your own mouth.

What does wise speech sound like? James explains: "The wisdom that comes from heaven is first of all pure; then peace-loving, considerate, submissive, full of mercy and good fruit, impartial and sincere" (James 3:17).

My husband's Aunt Iris was one of the wisest women I've ever known. She never conjugated a Greek or Hebrew verb or earned a college degree. She never went to college, drove a car, or looked at a computer screen. But she knew God and immersed herself in His presence continually. I'd often hear her singing, "I come to the garden alone, while the dew is still on the roses...And He walks with me, and He talks with me, and He tells me I am his own; and the joy we share as we tarry there, none other has ever known." Iris was a wise woman.

I believe wisdom has little to do with intelligence. I've often heard that the difference between a smart person and a wise person is that a smart person knows what to say and a wise person knows whether to say it or not.

I have known many highly educated fools. Apparently, so did the apostle Paul. He wrote, "Do not deceive yourselves. If any of you think you are wise by the standards of this age, you should become 'fools' so that you may become wise. For the wisdom of this world is foolishness in God's sight" (1 Corinthians 3:18-19).

There is nothing wrong with knowledge, but there is a vast difference between wisdom and knowledge. Wisdom is the God-given ability to apply knowledge correctly. "A wise person makes decisions based on the understanding that God and his time-honored principles are the only sure foundation for life. A foolish person does not act on the foundation of a reverence for God and instead lives recklessly for selfish gain."[3]

"Like a gold ring in a pig's snout is a beautiful woman who shows no discretion" (Proverbs 11:22). I call that the original Miss Piggy. No matter how beautiful a woman is on the outside, a lack of discretion on the inside will mar the view.

Here's a general rule of thumb: If in doubt, leave it out. In other words, if you are not sure if you should say something, then don't.

TIMING IS EVERYTHING

When Steven was about seven years old, we went snow skiing. For hours I instructed him in how to stand up, ski down, and get up once he fell. In his frustration, Steven fell down and fell down and fell down. He was not getting the hang of it at all. *What's the problem?* I wondered. Then I found out. It was me.

"Mom," Steven cried, "if you just quit telling me what to do, I think I could get it."

"Fine!" I said. "Go ahead and do it your way!"

And you know what? He did. Thirty minutes later Steven was cruising down the slopes with ease. My continued instruction had been a hindrance to Steven working out the maneuvers on his own. It started out being a skiing lesson for Steven, but it ended up being a parenting lesson for me.

Sometimes the most powerful words are the ones we withhold. "There is a time for everything, and a season for every activity under the heavens...a time to be silent and a time to speak" (Ecclesiastes 3:1,7).

In the Bible, Esther is a wonderful example of a wise woman who knew that timing was crucial. Under the influence of the evil Haman, King Xerxes issued a decree that the Hebrew people be destroyed. However, the king didn't know that Queen Esther was one of them.

After much prayer, fasting, and deliberation, Esther went before the king to make a petition. It was an important request because the entire Hebrew nation was at stake. When the king asked her to make her request, she didn't grovel at his feet and beg for her people to be spared. Rather, she calmly invited him to dinner. The timing wasn't right. When the king attended the soiree the following evening, she didn't grovel at his feet and beg for her people to be spared. Once again, she invited him to dinner the following evening. The timing still wasn't right.

At the second dinner party, the king offered Esther yet a third opportunity to make her request. Finally, Esther revealed evil Haman's plot to annihilate the entire Hebrew nation, which included her as well. But here's a lesson among the drama. Esther had a very important request for the king. And yet it was all about timing. Sure, she could have made the request the first time she approached the king and he extended the golden scepter in approval. She could have offered her petition at the first dinner party when he offered her anything she desired, "up to half the kingdom" (Esther 5:3). But there was something in Esther's spirit that caused her to wait. The timing wasn't right.

Even though the Bible doesn't tell us directly, I believe Esther was listening to God. Because of her obedience, the entire Hebrew nation was saved. That is the power of a woman's words offered at the right time.

A large part of discerning when to be silent and when to speak is learning how to listen well. "Listening is midwifery, the work of someone willing to allow another to labor in pain and joy, who refuses to numb these precious things by coming too quickly to re-assure or make everything right. Listening to another person enables, gently facilitates birth…to help another who has lost hope to come to light through the process."[4] That includes listening to the person we're talking to as well as listening to God.

The Bible teaches:

[She] who guard[s] [her] lips preserve[s] [her life], but [she] who speak[s] rashly will come to ruin (Proverbs 13:3).

Do you see [a woman] who speaks in haste? There is more hope for a fool than for [her] (Proverbs 29:20).

[She who] answer[s] before listening—that is [her] folly and shame (Proverbs 18:13).

Everyone should be quick to listen, slow to speak and slow to become angry, because [woman's] anger does not produce the righteousness that God desires (James 1:19-20).

Ralph Waldo Emerson said, "A friend is a person with whom I may be sincere. Before him, I may think aloud."[5] In order to think aloud, someone has to be on the receiving end listening. There is a difference between truly listening and waiting for your turn to talk. A true listener...

Does not interrupt. Interrupting communicates, "What I have to say is more important than what you have to say."

Invites you to tell her more with words such as, "How did that make you feel?"

Affirms the speaker with words such as, "Yes, I see." A true listener pays attention not only to the words of the speaker, but also to the emotions that drive the words.

Does not offer a solution unless asked. "What you should do is..." This minimizes the person's problems and makes it appear that you have all the answers. In other words, the person feels worse than before they confided the problem.

Does not judge. For example, "That was a terrible way to act."

Does not argue. It is better to be kind than correct when listening to someone pour out her heart.

Listens for the emotions behind the words in addition to the words themselves. "That must have been painful for you."

In Dietrich Bonhoeffer's classic work *Life Together*, he wrote this about the ministry of listening:

> The first service that one owes to others in the fellowship consists in listening to them. Just as love of God begins with listening to His Word, so the beginning of love for the brethren is learning to listen to them. It is God's love for us that He not only gives us His Word but also lends us His ear. So it is His work that we do for our brother when we learn to listen to him. Christians…forget that listening can be a greater service than speaking.
>
> Many people are looking for an ear that will listen. They do not find it among Christians, because these Christians are talking when they should be listening. But he who can no longer listen to his brother will soon no longer be listening to God either; he will be doing nothing but prattle in the presence of God too. Anyone who thinks that his time is too valuable to spend keeping quiet will eventually have no time for God and his brother, but only for himself and his own follies.[6]

Jesus was a master listener. He never interrupted but asked good questions that helped people come to their own conclusions. He listened to the lame man lying by the pool, the leper languishing by the side of the road, the children clamoring around His feet, the desperate father pleading for his child's sanity, the friend questioning His true identity, and His Father giving Him daily instructions.

Some of the most poignant moments of Jesus's arrest were the silent ones. "He was oppressed and afflicted, yet he did not open his mouth; he was led like a lamb to the slaughter, and as a sheep before its shearers is silent, so he did not open his mouth" (Isaiah 53:7). And for you and me, some of our most powerful moments will be the ones in which we remain silent. Some of the most powerful words are the ones that are withheld.

13

The Bucket Principle

Come to me, all you who are weary and burdened,
and I will give you rest. Take my yoke upon you and learn from me,
for I am gentle and humble in heart, and you will find rest for
your souls. For my yoke is easy and my burden is light.

Matthew 11:28-30

We've looked at the many ways we can use our words to speak life into other people, to pour positive words into the hearts of those in our slice of life. But what if you're the one who needs the encouraging words, and you feel like you have nothing to give? I get it, I've been there too. God reminded me about what I need to do during those times when Steve and I made a somewhat dangerous decision on a vacation adventure.

We were on a cruise ship that docked at Cozumel Island. Steve and I walked off the plank into the hustle and bustle of locals waiting to entertain the new batch of tourists entering their bit of paradise.

"Let's get away from all the congestion," Steve suggested. "I want to see the unspoiled part of the island."

So we rented a small motorcycle, secured our helmets, and set out on an adventure.

"This road goes around the island," the renter explained. "Just stay on this road, and you will return."

Off we went to circle the beautiful island of Cozumel. It wasn't too long before civilization lay behind and the open road promised romantic scenery. Deserted white, sandy beaches hugged the road on the right. But after several miles, the landscape changed. Lush palms transformed into bare, craggy branches. Seagulls were replaced with dark, menacing vultures, and the terrain was piled high with debris of a massive garbage dump. No longer was this a peaceful ride through paradise. We were lone travelers on the back side of the island, and we suddenly realized we were unprotected prey for any number of predators watching for unsuspecting tourists who had lost their way. The stench of the island's landfill was overwhelming, and the circling birds of prey seemed waiting for us to run out of gas.

"Can't this thing go any faster?" I cried.

"I've got it wide open," Steve assured. "I'm trying to get us out of here as fast as I can."

I am delighted to report that we did make it back to civilization. We threw off those helmets and ran across the plank to the ship as fast as our shaky legs could take us. In a matter of three hours, we had gone full circle. Paradise, garbage heap, paradise.

Why do I tell you this story? Because there are some days when I feel as though I am on the back side of the island. I look and there's garbage everywhere. I sense vultures circling the air just waiting for me to fall so they can pick me apart. The breeze is filled with stench, and paradise is filled with parasites.

Then I wonder, *How can I use my words to encourage and empower others when I feel so discouraged and empty myself? How can I give to others when I feel so depleted? I'm on the back side of the island, and I'm the one who needs encouragement!* Then God begins to show me ways to get filled up so that I can again pour out.

THE BUCKET PRINCIPLE

A sign was posted on a telephone pole by the grocery store: "LOST DOG with three legs, blind in left eye, missing right ear, tail broken, and recently castrated. Answers to the name of Lucky!"

Perhaps you feel just about as "lucky" as that lost dog. Hobbling along. Impaired vision. Broken tail. Well, you get the picture. There was a woman in the Bible who also felt like she was out of luck and had nothing to give. But then God showed her how to fill up so that she could pour out. Her story is found in 1 Kings 17, and it begins with a man named Elijah.

Elijah was a good prophet who gave some bad news to a king named Ahab: "As the LORD, the God of Israel, lives, whom I serve, there will be neither dew nor rain in the next few years except at my word" (1 Kings 17:1). God knew that news would not go over very well with the king, so He told Elijah to flee eastward and hide in the Kerith Ravine east of the Jordan. For several months, Elijah drank from the brook and ate bread and meat delivered by ravens that God miraculously sent to feed him. Only kings could afford to eat meat every day; God provided the very best for His servant.

Sometime later, the brook dried up. Now, if God could supply meat and bread every day, He could have easily provided water. But God had a different idea. He sent Elijah to Zarephath to a Gentile widow who needed a miracle in her life.

Elijah did as the Lord said and traveled to this widow's home. But he didn't find a woman with abundance ready to provide sustenance. What he found was a destitute widow who had given up on life. When Elijah arrived, she was stooping to the ground picking up sticks and placing them in a bundle.

"Excuse me," Elijah called, "could you please bring me a cup of water?"

As she turned to fetch the traveler a cup to quench his thirst, he continued. "Oh, and can you bring me a piece of bread?"

With this request, I imagine the woman sarcastically grumbled, *And would you like a lamb chop to go along with it?*

"I don't have any bread—only a handful of flour in a jar and a little oil in a jug," she said. "I am gathering a few sticks to take home and make a meal for myself and my son, that we may eat it—and die" (1 Kings 17:12).

Now that was a discouraged, empty woman! But Elijah had good news for her.

"Don't be afraid," Elijah said. "Go home and do as you have said. But first make a small loaf of bread for me from what you have and bring it to me, and then make something for yourself and your son. For this is what the LORD, the God of Israel says: 'The jar of flour will not be used up and the jug of oil will not run dry until the day the LORD gives rain on the land'" (verses 13-14).

She went away and did what Elijah had told her.

Can't you just see this woman taking the last bit of flour and oil to make Elijah a meal? *What does it matter? I'm going to die anyway. So what if it is one day early.*

She emptied her flour bowl and oil jar, took a little cake to Elijah, and returned home. As she goes to wash the dirty dishes, she picks up the jar and the jug and her senses are jostled! The jar is full of flour, and the jug is full to the brim with oil. She was an empty woman, but as she took what little she had to offer encouragement to another, God filled her up.

I call this the Bucket Principle. I believe that each of us is given a bucket of encouragement that we are to pour onto those around us. As we dip out of our bucket and pour onto others, God miraculously fills it back up.

There *are* those who have buckets that are running a bit low or even close to empty. Maybe they haven't had many deposits from other people lately, or maybe their bucket has a leak. In order to try to fill their bucket, they dip out of someone else's bucket with a cutting word here or a degrading comment there. But you know what? You can never get your bucket filled by dipping out of someone else's. You can only get your bucket filled by dipping out of your own and sharing the encouragement with others. When you give from your bucket of encouragement, God will pour more back into yours. After Naomi had lost her husband and her two sons, she said, "I went away full, but the LORD has brought me back empty" (Ruth 1:21). What she didn't realize was that God had provided Ruth to dip out of her bucket to fill Naomi's up again. In the meantime, God kept Ruth's filled to the brim. He filled Naomi's bucket, He filled the widow's bucket, and He will fill yours as well.

Jesus said, "Give, and it will be given to you. A good measure, pressed down, shaken together and running over, will be poured into your lap. For with the measure you use, it will be measured to you" (Luke 6:38). Many times we place a lid on our bucket of encouragement. *I don't have enough to give to someone else. I am drained dry,* we moan. However, when we give, even in our emotional emptiness, God fills us back up.

He also taught, "Remember this: Whoever sows sparingly will also reap sparingly, and whoever sows generously will also reap generously" (2 Corinthians 9:6). Do you want your bucket of encouragement and positive words to be filled to overflowing? Then begin dipping out and pouring into the lives of others. The same Jesus who multiplied five loaves of bread and two tiny fish into a feast to feed 5,000 men plus women and children (Matthew 14:15-21) will take your simple words of encouragement and multiply them to feed *your* hungry soul.

We play a game with our friends called Shanghai. Each player is dealt 11 cards, and the object of the game is to play your cards on other players' cards. While most games are about accumulating points, in this game the first person to give all the cards away wins.

That's how it is with the game of life. The more encouraging words you give away, the more you win! Some words are people specific, but some are wild cards and can be played anywhere. "Thank you," "Please," "I'm sorry," "You did that so well," "I appreciate that." Go ahead. Try it. You'll be amazed at the power you have to change the course of someone's day, and that someone can be you!

What happened to the woman from Zarephath? "For the jar of flour was not used up and the jug of oil did not run dry, in keeping with the word of the LORD spoken by Elijah" (1 Kings 17:16).

PRAISE OPENS HEAVEN'S SPIGOT

It's easy to feel guilty for feeling so empty, since we know in our knower that we've really been blessed with so much. But even David in the Bible had times when he felt that he had nothing to give.

While King Saul was still on his throne, God chose David to be Saul's successor. This didn't sit too well with the king, and he attempted to kill David before the crown could be placed on his handsome head. The young David, who earlier had bravely charged the Philistine giant Goliath, now ran for his life. The one place Saul didn't think David would hide was among the Philistines, whom he had previously shamed. So that is exactly where David hid...the briar patch, so to speak.

By this time, David had a 600-man army gathered round him. Each man brought his wife and children to live in the camp. The ragtag team of outcasts became David's kingdom for a time.

One day while David and his men were off fighting a battle, another group of people, the Amalekites, invaded their camp and took their wives and children captive. When David and his men returned home, they found empty beds, smoldering fires, and the haunting absence of familiar voices.

The men wept until they had no more strength to weep or energy for recourse. Rather than devise a rescue plan, they turned their anger on their leader and threatened to stone him. Hurting people often hurt people, and they were looking for someone to blame.

Can you imagine how David must have felt? His previous employer was trying to kill him (he had worked in Saul's palace), his best friends had turned against him, and his wife and children had been taken captive or possibly killed. Where was he to turn? How could he encourage his men when he had nothing left to give?

There was only one place to turn...to God.

"David found strength in the LORD his God" (1 Samuel 30:6). Friend, sometimes to God is the only place we can go. Isn't it a pity that we wait until God is our last resort rather than our first line of defense? Yes, God has called us to live in community with other believers, but sometimes He wants us all to Himself.

When you feel you have nothing to give—that you're as empty as a drained well—start praising God and watch for Him to fill you up. That's what David did in the psalms. Many times while he was on the run, he penned psalms about how depressed and distressed he was. But then part way through his lament, he reminded himself of God's character and His ways. In other words, David gave himself a good talkin' to; he talked to himself about himself. Once he remembered God's lavish love for him and powerful arm working for him, his mood lifted. As he praised God in his emptiness, God filled him with His bigness. Let's take a look at just one example:

> As the deer pants for the water brooks,
> So my soul pants for You, O God.
> My soul thirsts for God, for the living God;
> When shall I come and appear before God?
> My tears have been my food day and night,
> While *they* say to me all day long, "Where is your God?"
> These things I remember and I pour out my soul within me.
> For I used to go along with the throng and lead them in procession to the house of God,
> With the voice of joy and thanksgiving, a multitude keeping festival (Psalm 42:1-4 NASB).

Hear the emptiness? *My soul pants for You. My soul thirsts for You. I used to lead the people in praise with a voice of joy, but not anymore.* Then David begins to use his words to talk to himself.

> *Why are you in despair, O my soul?*
> *And why have you become disturbed within me?*
>
> *Hope in God, for I shall again praise Him*
> *For the help of His presence.*
>
> *O my God, my soul is in despair within me;*
> *Therefore I remember You from the land of the Jordan*
> *And the peaks of Hermon, from Mount Mizar.*
> *Deep calls to deep at the sound of Your waterfalls;*
> *All Your breakers and Your waves have rolled over me.*
> *The LORD will command His lovingkindness in the daytime;*
> *And His song will be with me in the night,*
> *A prayer to the God of my life* (42:5-8).

Oh, do you hear God pouring into David's emptiness? The sound of God's waterfall. The breakers and the waves rolling over him. Surrounding him. Covering him. Filling him.

Jesus experienced discouragement on many occasions. On the night before His arrest, He left the company of His closest friends and "going a little farther, he fell with his face to the ground and prayed" (Matthew 26:39). At that point, Jesus needed more than His friends. He needed His Dad. Likewise, there will be times when we are desperate, and the words of mere humans are not enough. We need to go to a deeper place, a place alone with God, and let His words encourage us.

When we feel that we are on the back side of the island, we need to make sure we don't get off the motorcycle and park by the garbage heap. Keep going! Begin using your words to praise God and fuel the vehicle that will get you out of the dumps.

14

Profound Possibilities

The tongue of a man (woman) is his (her) sword
and affective speech stronger than all fighting.

AUTHOR UNKNOWN

isten...do you hear them? Open your front door and step out into the world. They swarm around and surround us on every side. Small ones with tremendous impact. Large ones looming and misunderstood. Swirling. Churning. Spinning. Burning. Listen, do you hear them? One of the mightiest forces in all creation...words.

God has given each of us a priceless gift with profound possibilities to impact the world we live in for good. How will we use this gift? How will our words be received?

An artist discovered the profound possibilities he possessed as he painted the portrait of a homeless man. He came to the park every day at the same time, when the light was just right, positioning his easel and paints under the same familiar shade tree. It was his favorite spot to work and the perfect setting in which to satisfy his passion for painting. A talented and sensitive man, he specialized in portraits, skillfully drawing out the inner qualities of his subject. He watched the people strolling by for hours, searching for just the right face to paint. He loved the way each face told many different stories; some were filled with joy and others with pain and sadness, but all were filled with life.

A homeless man sitting across the path caught the artist's eye. Thinking of God's handiwork in every human being, he resolved to paint the man as he imagined he could be. With the last stroke, he breathed a sigh of satisfaction, a contented smile spreading across his face. It was done. And it was some of his best work. The artist then called the man over to see the painting. "Is this me?" the homeless man asked. "That is the 'you' I see!" replied the artist. The man stared at the painting silently. Finally, with tears in his eyes, he softly declared, "If that's the man you see in me, then that's the man I'm going to be!"

Each and every day we are painting portraits of the people we meet. We may not be holding a paintbrush and splashing brilliant colors on canvas, but we are painting pictures with the words we speak. Men, women, boys, and girls are seeing themselves in our words. Many are determining their worth, their potential, and even their destiny by what they hear others say about them.

Will your words reflect the fact that each individual is "God's masterpiece" (Ephesians 2:10 NLT), "chosen…and dearly loved" (Colossians 3:12), "fearfully and wonderfully made" (Psalm 139:14)? You have that potential, you know. It's right under your nose.

YOU ARE BECOMING
WHOM YOU ARE GOING TO BE

So, here we are at the end of our journey, and the question remains: How will we use our words…one of God's most incredible gifts to mankind? Will we invest them wisely or squander them foolishly? Will we use them to build up others or tear them down? Oh, the power we possess to bless those around us and encourage them to be all that God has created them to be. Our very words have the potential to change the course of a day…to change the course of a life.

Day by day we are becoming whom we are going to be. Let me close with words that have had a great impact on my life as I ponder the future and the woman who will one day look back at me in the mirror.

YOU'LL MEET AN
OLD LADY ONE DAY

You are going to meet an old lady someday. Down the road 10, 20, 30 years—she's waiting for you. You will catch up to her. What kind of old lady are you going to meet?

She may be a seasoned, soft, and gracious lady. A lady who has grown old gracefully, surrounded by a host of friends—friends who call her blessed because of what her life has meant to them. Or she may be a bitter, disillusioned, dried-up, cynical old buzzard without a good word for anyone or anything—soured, friendless, and alone. The kind of old lady you will meet will depend entirely upon you.

She will be exactly what you make of her, nothing more, nothing less. It's up to you. You will have no one else to credit or blame. Every day, in every way, you are becoming more and more like that old lady. You are getting to look more like her, think more like her, and talk more like her. You are becoming her. If you live only in terms of what you are getting out of life, the old lady gets smaller, drier, harder, crabbier, more self-centered. Open your life to others. Think in terms of what you can give and your contribution to life, and the old lady grows larger, softer, kinder, greater.

These little things, seemingly so unimportant now—attitudes, goals, ambitions, desires—are adding up inside where you cannot see them, crystallizing in your heart and mind. The point is, these things don't always show up immediately. But they will—sooner than you think. Someday they will harden into that old lady; nothing will be able to soften or change them then.

The time to take care of that old lady is right now. Today. Examine your motives, attitudes, goals. Check up on her. Work her over now while she is still pliable, still in a formative condition. Then you will be much more likely to meet a lovely, gracious old lady at the proper time.[1]

Notes

CHAPTER 2—GOD'S INCREDIBLE GIFT

1. Elizabeth Silance Ballard, "Three Letters from Teddy," *Home Life*, March 1976. Used with permission.
2. *ESV Study Bible* (Wheaton, IL: Crossway Bibles, 2008), footnote for James 3:3-6, 2395.
3. Ibid.
4. Bill Gabbert, "Analyzing the Fire That Burned into Gatlinburg," *Wildfire Today*, December 5, 2016, wildfiretoday.com/2016/12/05/analyzing-the-fire-that-burned-into-gatlinburg/161203-story.html.
5. Spiros Zodhiates, as quoted in *The Tale of the Tardy Ox Cart*, compiled by Charles Swindoll (Nashville, TN: Word Publishing, 1998), 575.
6. Charles Swindoll, *Encourage Me* (Grand Rapids, MI: Zondervan Publishing House, 1992), 19.
7. William Barclay, "The Letter to the Hebrews," *The Daily Study Bible* (Edinburgh, Scotland: St. Andrews Press, 1955), 173-78.
8. *Strong's Exhaustive Concordance of the Bible* (Gordonsville, TN: Dugan Publishers, Inc., 1984), 6310.
9. Adapted from Sister Helen P. Mrosla, O.S.F., "All the Good Things." Originally published in *Proteus*, Spring 1991. Reprinted by permission as edited and published by Reader's Digest in October 1991.

CHAPTER 3—A WOMAN'S LIFE-CHANGING POTENTIAL

1. Carol Kline with Jean Harper, "The Wind Beneath Her Wings," *Chicken Soup for the Woman's Soul* (Deerfield Beach, FL: Health Communications, Inc., 1996). Used by permission.
2. Alan Loy McGinnis, *Bringing Out the Best in People* (Minneapolis, MN: Augsburg Publishing House, 1985), 71-72.
3. Carolyn's story is found in *Treasures of Encouragement* by Sharon W. Betters (Phillipsburg, NJ: P&R Publishing, 1996), 160-61.
4. Adapted from "When a Stranger Called, He Answered," by Mark Washburn, *The Charlotte Observer*, E1, December 9, 2006.

CHAPTER 4—BIG IMPACT ON LITTLE PEOPLE:
THE POWER OF A WOMAN'S WORDS TO HER CHILDREN

1. "Mama's Plan," is reprinted with permission from *Guideposts* magazine.

2. https://kidblog.org/home/the-power-of-words-positive-vs-negative/.

   Or Neil Anderson, *Victory Over the Darkness* (Ventura, CA: Regal Books, 1990), 63.

3. William Barclay, "Letters to the Galatians and Ephesians," *The Daily Study Bible* (Edinburgh, Scotland: St. Andrews Press, 1962), 211.

4. https://www.verywellfit.com/support-athletes-for-success-3120701.

5. "Kids and Tech: The Evolution of Today's Digital Natives," *Influence Central*, accessed June 25, 2019, influence-central.com/kids-tech-the-evolution-of-todays-digital-natives/.

6. Mabel Bartlett and Sophia Baker, *Mothers—Makers of Men* (New York: Exposition Press, 1952), 92.

7. "I Don't Believe a Word of It" from Alice Gray, *More Stories for the Heart* (Sisters, OR: Multnomah Publishers, 1997), 46.

CHAPTER 5—THE DRIPPING FAUCET OR THE REFRESHING
WELL: THE POWER OF A WOMAN'S WORDS TO HER HUSBAND

1. Carolyn Custis James, *When Life and Beliefs Collide* (Grand Rapids, MI: Zondervan Publishing House, 2001), 181.

2. Nancy Anderson, "I Am a Woman—Hear Me Roar," 2004. Used with permission.

3. From the Billy Graham Evangelistic Association, *Billy Graham, God's Ambassador* (Nashville, TN: Word Publishing Group, 1999).

4. Ibid.

5. www.bgea.org/News_Article.asp?ArticleID=163.

6. Taken from Ed Wheat, *Love Life for Every Couple* (Grand Rapids, MI: Zondervan Publishing House, 1980), 177.

7. Excerpted from Sharon Jaynes, *Becoming the Woman of His Dreams* (Eugene, OR: Harvest House Publishers, 2005), 42-44, 69-73.

8. Jack Cranfield and Mark Victor Hansen, "Encouragement," from *Chicken Soup for the Soul* (Deerfield Beach, FL: Health Communications, Inc., 1993), 213.

CHAPTER 6—COME SIT BY ME: THE POWER
OF A WOMAN'S WORDS TO HER FRIENDS

1. Charles Caldwell Ryrie, *Ryrie Study Bible* (Chicago, IL: Moody Publishers, 1977), 1778.

2. Ann Hibbard, *Treasured Friends* (Grand Rapids, MI: Baker Books, 1997), 16-17.

3. Dale Carnegie, *How to Win Friends and Influence People* (New York: Simon and Schuster, 1981), 52.

CHAPTER 7—CHEERING FROM THE SIDELINES: THE POWER
OF A WOMAN'S WORDS TO HER ADULT CHILDREN

1. https://www.focusonthefamily.com/parenting/parenting-roles/phases-of-parenthood.

2. http://www.pursuegod.org/parenting-in-stages/.

3. https://www.focusonthefamily.com/parenting/parenting-roles/phases-of-parenthood.

4. https://www.nytimes.com/2012/03/24/your-money/why-people-remember-negative-events -more-than-positive-ones.html.

5. http://biblehub.com/hebrew/1692.htm.

6. Sharon Jaynes, *Lovestruck* (Nashville, TN: Thomas Nelson, 2019), 56.

CHAPTER 8—ESPECIALLY THESE: THE POWER OF A WOMAN'S WORDS TO FELLOW BELIEVERS

1. Kenneth Barker, general ed., *NIV Study Bible* (Grand Rapids, MI: Zondervan Publishing House, 1995), 336.

2. Kenneth L. Barker and John R. Kohlenberger III, *Zondervan NIV Commentary Volume 1: Old Testament* (Grand Rapids, MI: Zondervan Publishing House, 1994), 198.

CHAPTER 9—THE WOMAN IN THE CHECKOUT LINE: THE POWER OF A WOMAN'S WORDS TO THE WORLD

1. Adapted from Dan Clark, "Are You God?" in *Chicken Soup for the Woman's Soul* (Deerfield Beach, FL: Health Communications, Inc., 1996), 27.

2. Alan Loy McGinnis, *The Friendship Factor* (Minneapolis, MN: Augsburg Publishing House, 1979), 101-02.

3. David Jeremiah, *The Power of Encouragement* (Sisters, OR: Multnomah Publishers, 1997), 13.

4. C.S. Lewis, *The Four Loves* (New York: Harcourt Brace, 1960), 3.

5. This quote is often attributed to Theodore Doystoyevsky but wasn't found as such in a Google book search.

6. Richard H. Seume, *Shoes for the Road* (Chicago, IL: Moody Press, 1974), 117.

CHAPTER 10—YOU'RE NOT IN THIS ALONE

1. Joann C. Webster and Karen Davis, eds., *A Celebration of Women* (Southlake, TX; Watercolor Books, 2001), 167.

2. https://www.visualthesaurus.com/cm/wc/seven-ways-to-write-a-better-speech/.

CHAPTER 11—THE GRAVEYARD OF GRUMBLING AND THE LIFE FORCE OF GRATITUDE

1. *The New Lexicon Webster's Dictionary of the English Language* (New York: Lexicon Publications, 1990), 425.

2. Joshua Rothman, "A Few Notes on Grumbling," *New Yorker*, January 22, 2015, www.newyorker .com/culture/cultural-comment/notes-grumbling (accessed July 14, 2015).

3. Ibid.

4. https://www.youtube.com/watch?v=RPaJbpEl_FI Audio Book, *The Squeaky Wheel* by Guy Winch, PhD.

5. Ibid.

6. Adapted from *The Hiding Place* by Corrie Ten Boom (Old Tappan, NJ: A Bantam book published by Fleming Revell, 1971, 1974).

7. Sarah Ban Breathnach, *The Simple Abundance Journal of Gratitude* (New York: Warner Books, Inc., 1996), 2-3.

8. Sharon Jaynes, *Take Hold of the Faith You Long For* (Grand Rapids, MI: Baker Books, 2016), 200-01.

9. Henry Ward Beecher, *Life Thoughts, Gathered from the Extemporaneous Discourses of Henry Ward Beecher* (New York: Sheldon, 1860), 115.

10. Jean Baptiste Massieu, quoted in Robert A. Emmons, *Thanks! How the New Science of Gratitude Can Make You Happier* (New York: Houghton Mifflin, 2007), 89.

11. William Mounce, gen. ed., *Mounce's Complete Expository Dictionary of Old and New Testament Words*, (Grand Rapids, MI: Zondervan Publishing, 2006), 387.

12. Erasmus, quoted in Andy Zubko, *Treasure of Spirit Wisdom* (New Delhi, India: Morilal Banarsidass, 2003), 2109.

13. Charles R. Swindoll, *Strengthening Your Grip* (Brentwood, TN: Worthy Books, 2015), 227.

14. Melody Beattie, "Gratitude," MelodyBeattie.com, December 31, 2017, https://melodybeattie.com/gratitude-2/.

CHAPTER 12–THE MELODY OF SILENCE

1. Charles L. Allen, *God's Psychiatry* (Grand Rapids, MI: Fleming H. Revell Company, 1953), 75.

2. Karen Ehman, *Keep.It.Shut* (Grand Rapids, MI: Zondervan, 2015), 39.

3. Karol Ladd, *The Power of a Positive Woman* (West Monroe, LA: Howard Publishing Co., Inc., 2002), 75.

4. Marlee Alex, "An Open Window," *Virtue* (May/June 1994), 4.

5. Every effort has been made to trace the source of this quotation.

6. Dietrich Bonhoeffer, *Life Together*, trans. John W. Doberstein (New York: Harper & Brothers, 1954), 97-98.

CHAPTER 14–PROFOUND POSSIBILITIES

1. Mary Southerland, *Sandpaper People* (Eugene, OR: Harvest House Publishers, 2005), 13-14.

About the Author

Sharon Jaynes is an international inspirational speaker and Bible teacher for women's conferences and events. She is the past vice president and radio cohost for Proverbs 31 Ministries and current writer for their Encouragement for Today devotions. Sharon is also the cofounder of Girlfriends in God, Inc. She is also a best selling author of several books, including *Enough: Silencing the Lies that Steal Your Confidence*; *Lovestruck: God's Design for Romance, Marriage, & Sexual Intimacy from the Song of Solomon*; and *Praying for Your Husband from Head to Toe: A Daily Guide for Scripture-Based Prayer*. Her books have been translated into several foreign languages and impacted women all around the globe. Sharon and her husband, Steve, live in North Carolina and have one grown son, Steven, and his amazing wife, Emily.

You can visit with Sharon on her blog at

www.sharonjaynes.com.

You can also follow Sharon at

www.Facebook.com/sharonjaynes

www.Facebook.com/ThePrayingWivesClub

www.Pinterest.com/sharonjaynes

www.Instagram.com/sharonejaynes

To learn more about Sharon's books and speaking ministry or to inquire about having Sharon speak at your next event, visit www.sharon jaynes.com.

THE POWER OF A WOMAN'S WORDS
BIBLE STUDY AND DISCUSSION GUIDE

Go Deeper

This companion study guide to *The Power of a Woman's Words* offers biblical instruction and practical tools to help you discover the power of words to change the course of your day and even your life.

Your words hold immense power. They echo in hearts and minds long after they are spoken. Your words can

- be encouraging and uplifting
- provide helpful instruction
- bring healing and comfort
- display loving-kindness

In this Bible study and discussion guide, Sharon Jaynes walks you alongside women of the Bible—women like Rachel who shaped her son's character, Sarai who influenced her husband's choices, and Elizabeth who boosted her friend's confidence—to help you discover life-changing ways to shape your words and their impact.

Perfect for personal or group use.